SUNSET LODGE *in* GEORGETOWN

The Story of a Madam

DAVID GREGG HODGES

THE History PRESS

Published by The History Press
Charleston, SC
www.historypress.com

First published 2019

Manufactured in the United States

ISBN 9781467143660

Library of Congress Control Number: 2019943518

Sunset Lodge, the worst kept secret in South Carolina history. The perfect example of "hide in plain sight."
—*Philip Edward Wilson, co-owner, Control Management, Inc., Columbia, South Carolina*

David Hodges, a wonderfully canny storyteller, brings to bear his wit and human generosity, along with a deep affection for South Carolina and a subtle understanding of her history, in this fascinating account of a shrewd and philanthropic madam with an electrifying clientele.
—*Joan Hinde Stewart, retired president of Hamilton College, Clinton, New York*

One of the best written articles I have read as pertains to Hazel and Sunset Lodge. The history more matches what old Georgetonians have told they knew.... The author has obviously interviewed people who had direct interactions versus relying on rumors and speculation.
—*Francis B. "Jeepy" Ford Jr., Georgetown, South Carolina, commenting on an article about this book in* Columbia Metropolitan *magazine*

This book is not as bad as I feared.
—*the author's pastor, Derek William Henry Thomas, First Presbyterian Church, Columbia, South Carolina*

David Hodges has carefully researched his subject and done innumerable interviews to provide readers with a more factual account of the legendary Sunset Lodge. It was once described as "Georgetown's own little United Way" due to madam Hazel Weisse's gifts of money for a new police car, a new fire truck and a myriad of municipal and county needs. This story of Sunset Lodge is like that eccentric relative we all have. We have to claim them, but none of us want to talk about them in polite company...but we can talk about David Hodges's book.
—*Lee Gordon Brockington, historian and author of* Pawleys Island: A Century of History and Photographs, *Georgetown, South Carolina*

David Hodges has put into print a story that has been talked about—sometimes only whispered about—in Georgetown County for generations. Beyond pulling together individual recollections that have only become more precious with the passage of time, he has given valuable perspective to the peculiar institution that was the Sunset Lodge.
—Charles Swenson, Coastal Observer, *Pawleys Island, South Carolina*

Now maybe he will get back to selling life insurance.
—*the author's wife, Susan Graybill Hodges, owner, The Happy Café, Columbia, South Carolina*

CONTENTS

AUTHOR'S NARRATIVE

I had a cousin who used to say, "This is a true story, but I am going to tell it anyway."[1] Many people have told me stories about the Sunset Lodge in Georgetown, South Carolina, and I believe many of the stories are true; I just do not know which ones. That is the challenge of an oral history of a brothel; no one kept records, no one took pictures and no one put the story of his visit to the Sunset Lodge in his journal. There are no written first-person accounts. The newspaper articles I read were, for the most part, embarrassingly romanticized versions of what the writer thought he or she should say about the "house of ill repute." They were complimentary in tone and cute in design. The first critical article I read about the Sunset Lodge was in a column written by Tom Rubillo in the *Georgetown Times*, published in 2006.[2]

The only book published about the Sunset Lodge was an entertaining 1994 novel by Rebecca Godwin titled *Keeper of the House*.[3] Becky only mentioned the name of the brothel once, and that was in the introduction. She weaved some of the Sunset Lodge stories she had heard into a plot that kept the reader's attention. The reader had no idea which stories allegedly were true, but that did not matter; the plot and the characters made the book a good read.

I have been asked many times what interested me in this subject, which is a back-handed way of asking why a conservative man, married forty-three years with four children and nine grandchildren, who is an elder at his conservative Presbyterian church, would do such a thing as stir up memories of an illegal and immoral facility on the coast of South Carolina. Simply, I was casting about for a topic to research for a paper I was to give to a club I am in, and I thought of writing a paper about the Sunset Lodge. The first person I asked about the historic brothel told me there are no published accounts, but he offered to tell me a couple of stories. He did, and they were wonderful. It quickly became obvious this was a storytelling project. I had to find people who would tell me stories that I could feed to other people who would tell me more stories. Since the Sunset Lodge closed fifty years ago, the older the storyteller, the better.

The Sunset Lodge closed in 1969, so most of the stories I heard during my research came from men and women in their seventies or eighties. Some folks have died since I talked to them, and I missed some who died before we had the opportunity to visit. There are people in Georgetown and Columbia who even now have wonderful stories about the Sunset Lodge or the madam, Hazel Weisse, who are unwilling to share those stories. A house of prostitution is a difficult subject. Some residents in Georgetown are sensitive to the history of a brothel in town, some men are embarrassed to have visited the Sunset Lodge and some people just believe it is wrong even to bring up this subject; they think I am glorifying prostitution. Happily, most everyone understands the Sunset Lodge is a fascinating slice of the history of South Carolina.

The dark side to the interesting and fun stories of the Sunset Lodge is the immorality. Hazel Weisse was engaging in destructive human behavior. How much pain did she create in families? How many relationships were damaged or destroyed by her actions? How many men violated their marital vows by traveling to the Sunset Lodge? How many men were consumed with guilt or discovered their association with a strange woman damaged intimacy with their own wives? I talked to dozens of people and heard countless stories about the Sunset Lodge, many of them hysterically funny, but I never heard of a family broken or of a child torn apart by the tension of fighting parents. Is it possible it never happened? Of course it happened. No one wants to share those stories; those stories cut too deep. They are too personal, too hurtful.

The closest I got to serious objections to Hazel and the Sunset Lodge is described in the narrative *Blemish*. A local man who acknowledged he profited from Hazel's presence in Georgetown said he had no real objection to her business but he objected to her serving minors. We are not talking about minors drinking alcohol; we are talking about a young man, a boy fourteen years old, who knocked on the back door of the Sunset Lodge with ten dollars in his hand and Hazel let him in as a customer of her brothel. It is outrageous and worthy of condemnation, and yet Hazel had no serious challenge to her presence in Georgetown for thirty-three years. A few ministers tried to get her place of business closed, and H.D. Bull, the rector of Prince George Winyah Parish, went to the grand jury every year to ask that the Sunset Lodge be shut down, but nothing ever happened.

Collecting stories about the Sunset Lodge became a hobby, a three-ring binder where references and stories and factoids went to be safe for someday in the future. The presentation to my club created invitations to present my paper to other clubs, all composed of groups of men. It was fun. I was invited to cool private properties, and I told stories. I kept collecting information, I kept interviewing old people and I kept getting referrals to others who were said to know something about the brothel.

One day, a female friend asked me to speak to her garden club, a group of women who meet for lunch at someone's home to hear a speaker talk about most anything, it seems, but gardening. I gathered my material and went to see them. One woman walked up to me before the meeting and asked that I tell it all, to not hold back. She wanted to hear the truth. Standing in the living room with about twenty women sitting on sofas and chairs and ottomans, I told them what I knew about the Sunset Lodge. I explained how much money is being made now in areas where prostitution is currently legal. The daughter of a friend of mine was attending an expensive university a few years ago. The daughter's roommate asked her if she wanted to go with her to a brothel in Nevada where she planned on working that summer. She could make enough money during the summer to pay her entire tuition for the year plus $10,000 for her bank account. There was a stunned silence in the room, and a woman about my age in the back asked, "Is it too late?"

Paige Sawyer is a professional photographer in Georgetown. He has served on the Georgetown City Council and he knows everyone in town. The fact of the Sunset Lodge being in Georgetown from 1936 until 1969 always has interested him, and he had hoped to write about the famous brothel one day. He and I discovered our common interest, and we communicate regularly. He became a good friend and the person without whom I could not have found the material I needed to write this book. He actively solicited people for us to interview and talked to some business owners for me and sent me compilations of what was said.

Woody Gruber was, until recently, a folk artist who lived in Georgetown. He made models of the fronts of homes and businesses to sell in Georgetown County and elsewhere. He used scraps of wood and bits of stuff to make his models. Dried pinecones often became trees. I took him a photograph of the Sunset Lodge and asked if he could make a model, and he did. I use it as a visual aid when I give presentations. The pinecones fall off, but otherwise, it works great.

One day, I talked to a friend in Columbia about my project in Georgetown. She is a university academic, and she told me I would not understand what went on in the Sunset Lodge until I talked to the African Americans who worked there—the women who changed the sheets, the women who cooked the food and the men who worked in the yard. I called Paige Sawyer, and within two weeks, he and I were sitting with Edna Knox, a retired schoolteacher who had worked as a dishwasher at the Sunset Lodge during the summers while she was in college at South Carolina State in Orangeburg. Edna reported a good experience washing dishes. She was paid in cash and did not have to work on Sundays. For her story, see "Dishwasher."

My greatest regret was not finding a retired sporting lady who agreed to be interviewed. I found two women, but neither would talk to me. And I understand why. These are old ladies. They have moved on, and they do not want to open that box. A local physician told me he had a patient who used to work at the Sunset Lodge, and I asked him to ask her if she would talk with me. I did not need her name or any information about her. I would submit my questions in writing or we could talk on the phone. He sent me a fax that said simply, "She specifically said no."

The other woman I found had married and moved not far away. Several people gave me her name, address and phone number, but when I asked for an introduction, no one would help me. Their relationship with the woman did not include knowing about her experiences at the Sunset Lodge. I finally wrote her a note and explained my purpose, and she never responded, so I let it drop.

Most of this book is composed of brief narratives. I talked to business owners on Front Street, customers of the Sunset Lodge, vendors who provided goods and services to Hazel and even random people who knew a good story. As I researched and reviewed old newspapers, deeds and wills and looked up dates of events, I began to understand which stories could be true and which stories were not possible. My narratives became clearer, crisper and more certain.

Stories about the Sunset Lodge are wonderful in their simplicity and ease of telling, but I heard many stories from men who insisted I not identify them as the storyteller. I learned to have a conversation with a storyteller and either take no notes or write down just a word or two to remind myself of the story when I returned to my car or the hotel room. Had I pulled out a tape recorder, many men would have fled the room. One man I did not know met me for lunch, and the first thing he said was he needed to know how I was going to use the information he had to tell me. I told him I had two goals in writing this book: not to embarrass myself and not to embarrass anyone else. He was satisfied and told me an amazing story that is described in one of the narratives.

The narratives in this book are stories I have heard and from research I have done. The confidentiality of the storytellers has been protected, sometimes by combining stories and sometimes by creating stories that fit the facts. My earliest reader was my brother Bob. I would write a narrative and send it to him by e-mail for his reaction and comments. He was extraordinarily kind and encouraging. He loved the stories and thought it amazing that I found these folks to interview. He liked the personalities of some, and he disliked others. It took me a long time to realize he thought I had transcripts of these interviews.

For example, a local business owner told me a fun story about a heating and air guy who went to the Sunset Lodge to install an air conditioner in a window and observed the same woman taking men upstairs while he worked. The punch line to the story was she made more money while he was there than he did. I had little to work with other than the punch line. Starting with the punch line and working backward, I created a story that fit the ending. Brother Bob thought I had talked to the heating and air guy, and when he found out there was no heating and air guy—at least no living heating and air guy—well, he felt betrayed. I was focused on the story, and he was focused on the person.

I have notes of interviews that corroborate other interviews, but some events happened too long ago to be told by the person himself or herself. The truth is Hazel Weisse was in business from 1936 until 1969, and most of the early vendors, customers and residents who would have a story to tell are long since dead. Some of the stories were told to me by a person who was retelling a story from a father or uncle. I confirmed the information I could confirm and wrote the narratives.

I have heard of women traveling from one brothel to another to work for six months to a year before moving to another town. Towns mentioned include Jacksonville, Savannah, Birmingham and Wilmington. I have even heard of a directory of brothels that would allow madams to call one another to request new women to replace the women who had left. The question of where the women came from and where they went has bothered me for years. Hazel went through a lot of women. She clearly wanted to keep her inventory fresh, which suggests she had plenty of repeat business. One man told me Hazel would get rid of a woman if a man asked for her twice; Hazel did not want romantic relationships in her brothel. However, another man told me some of the women stayed at the Sunset Lodge for years and men had their favorites.

How should I handle discrepancies in stories I hear? Some men said Hazel served alcohol and had a bar in the dining room.[1] Other men said there was no alcohol and maybe just some beer in the kitchen refrigerator. Some men said they used the Sunset Lodge as a club, hanging out and drinking and dancing with no pressure to "go upstairs" with a girl. Other men said men went there for one thing, got their business done and left; there was no sociality. It seems to me that as an oral history, one experience may not equal another. Hazel Weisse was in business for thirty-three years. She moved to Georgetown when Franklin Roosevelt was the president of the United States. She closed the Sunset Lodge during Richard Nixon's term. She aged from thirty-six to sixty-nine years old while in Georgetown. Everything changes over time, and Hazel would have changed as well. Acknowledging the weakness of the human memory, I still give credibility to the storytellers who contradicted one another regarding facts. It could well be that the facts changed, not the memories.

There was a handwritten list of phone numbers that was nailed to the wall next to Hazel's phone in the pantry. The couple who bought the Sunset Lodge building in early 1970 kept the list and gave it to me. All the numbers are local. I have identified the names and numbers of physicians, car dealers, drugstores, clothing stores, the cab company and the airport. There are no numbers of other madams. Did Hazel have a private book of names and phone numbers? How did she contact women who wanted to work for her? The most important person in Hazel's business was Tom Yawkey, the owner of the Boston Red Sox baseball team and of twenty thousand acres in Georgetown County. One could argue she moved to Georgetown because of Yawkey. She clearly knew him and was a friend. His phone number is not on that phone list. Perhaps she knew Yawkey's number by heart, or maybe there is or was another list.

Men have talked about how pretty and nice the women were at the Sunset Lodge, and yet, business owners and bankers on Front Street have described them as "regular girls," women who looked like every other young woman in town. How could that be? How did Hazel find these women who were supposed to be uniquely beautiful and sophisticated if they were traveling a route of brothels? I believe this dichotomy is part of the fantasy of the Sunset Lodge—maybe of any high-end brothel. Hazel dressed these women in expensive clothes and shoes, and they wore makeup and perfume. It is likely her customers did not go home to wives dressed as these women were dressed or who smelled like these women smelled. By the time Hazel's women got dressed for work, they looked nothing like what the men were used to. I believe Hazel's business model created an environment for the men to live their fantasies. The women were not lined up along the wall for men to choose; the women were dressed and sitting on two enormously long sofas in the living room. They were happy to visit with the men and even to dance to music from the jukebox. The men were made to feel comfortable staying in the living room and talking and never taking a woman upstairs. Men told me they often visited the Sunset Lodge to have a few drinks, dance with the girls and go home. If they chose a partner, she was, as Julia Roberts said in *Pretty Woman*,[5] a sure thing.

Could it be that Hazel interviewed women who showed up at the Sunset Lodge asking for a job? I take a stab at this question with the narrative "Sporting Lady." Multiple people told me the sporting ladies often were the wives of men in the military, particularly during World War II. One man told me of a woman who worked at the Sunset Lodge for six months every time her navy husband went to sea. I have my doubts; see what you think.

Hazel Weisse did not solicit men to do business with her, and she did not allow her employees to solicit men while on Front Street in Georgetown. She tightly controlled their movements. Prostitution in most cities involves women standing on street corners or lingering in hotel lobbies. The Sunset Lodge was not like that at all. Men knew where the Sunset Lodge was, and they went to Hazel. She decided who to let into her building when they knocked on the back door. I heard one story of a man who tried to sell Hazel advertising. She assured him she had no need to advertise.

There were three sheriffs in Georgetown County during the thirty-three years that Hazel Weisse owned a brothel in Georgetown, and while it is true no one arrested Hazel and padlocked her building, I am not as critical of the sheriffs as some. Getting rid of prostitution is like playing Whack-a-Mole. I can name at least six houses of prostitution in Florence, South Carolina, during the time Hazel was in Georgetown and another several brothels in Columbia, South Carolina. I have had conversations with people in Columbia who have told me with great accuracy where this brothel was or that brothel. I have read accounts of arrests for prostitution in multiple newspapers from every decade, including this decade. The sheriffs did the best they could managing an issue that would not go away.

There are some wonderfully interesting insights into human behavior that I explore through storytelling. Which of these stories happened? I heard many first-person stories that I believe to be true, but it is hard to know how true any story is after it has been told and repeated over seventy-five years. The intent of this book is to create a mosaic of stories that paint the larger picture of what happened in Georgetown and why it happened.

Consider the narrative "Robbery." I was told by a retired policeman that there were no behavior problems at the Sunset Lodge, that the madam Hazel Weisse controlled her business environment. I wondered what that control might look like. I also wanted to explain why men would go to the Sunset Lodge with no intention of hiring a sporting lady but to use the brothel as a social club, so I created a situation that created tension; well, you go read it.

I have heard some stories dozens of times and not the same way twice. The most famous of these stories is the man who was trapped one night at the Sunset Lodge with his wife sitting in a car outside waiting for him to come out. Many people in Georgetown know who the man was, and he was even telling the story on himself by the time he died; even so, I hear many versions as people edit what they are told before telling it to the next person. In "The Wife," I wrote the story from his wife's perspective.

I interviewed one man who told me a long, involved story about Hazel sending flowers to the cemetery for his dad's funeral and the resulting meeting of his mother and Hazel. I fell for this story hook, line and sinker. The man telling me the story went into great detail as to his mother's insistence that she thank Hazel Weisse in person for sending flowers to the cemetery and his efforts to dissuade her from going to see Hazel. He described the meeting of the two ladies in the backseat of his mom's car and excitedly told me the climax of the story when Hazel told her new friend that she did not expect her to speak to Hazel on the street and his mom's response that she would be honored to speak to Hazel whenever she saw her next.

I told that story in one of my Rotary Club talks, and I was approached by a friend a few months later who had been at the meeting. The friend gently explained that the story I told at Rotary sounded familiar, so he looked up a reference in the novel *Gone with the Wind*.[6] In Margaret Mitchell's classic book published in 1936, the prostitute Belle Watling has a conversation with Melanie Wilkes, and Melanie says she will acknowledge Belle when she passes her on the street, but Belle tells her not to.

It was then I remembered the *Gone with the Wind* paraphernalia in the house of my friend who told me the story. The man was a *Gone with the Wind* collector; he had *Gone with the Wind* posters, music sheets, statuettes, movie tickets, shot glasses, souvenir spoons, coffee cups, framed photographs and fan magazines. How much of his story was true and how much came from *Gone with the Wind?*

I had similar challenges with Becky Godwin's book, *Keeper of the House*. Her fiction is embedded in the minds of some of the folks in Georgetown, and I will occasionally listen to a story about the Sunset Lodge and realize halfway through that Becky's storytelling skill has taken root and someone is telling me a story from her book.

Nick Zeigler wrote a book about a Florence resident, Frank Barnwell, titled *Barnwell Blarney*,[7] that tells a story about the Sunset Lodge—one of the few times I found a published story about the famous brothel. The Zeigler family gave me permission to use Nick's story in this book, so it is quoted in its entirety. My title of the narrative is "Arc Light in a Whorehouse." Eugene N. "Nick" Zeigler was a state senator from Florence County, and he authored six books. The South Carolina History Room at the Florence County library is named for Nick Zeigler.

Stories about the Sunset Lodge came from the strangest sources and at the oddest times. The narrative "Fraternity Initiation" was told publicly at the end of a Rotary Club meeting by an attendee who had just heard me speak about the Sunset Lodge. The narrative "Christmas Eve" was told to me privately after a Bible study. The narrative "Pawleys Island Trip" was told to me innocently by a gentleman who simply was explaining how difficult the trip was from Columbia to the beach during the World War II gas rationing. This gentleman will be horrified when he reads how I gave him the salacious intent to visit the Sunset Lodge as his reason for his trip to Pawleys. The narrative "Girl Scout" was told by a woman who took it back when she realized I might put the story in my book. Ah, too late!

I love Georgetown County, South Carolina. The town of Georgetown is the third oldest in South Carolina after Charleston and Beaufort. Georgetown is a coastal town with a deep-water harbor and easy access to visitors by water. Brothels and port towns go together, as do brothels and military bases. Georgetown had the Sunset Lodge for thirty-three years, and Hazel's presence was so powerful and pervasive that here we are at the fiftieth anniversary of the closing of the Sunset Lodge and people still are telling stories and marveling at her influence, not only in Georgetown but in the rest of South Carolina as well.

Georgetown County contains treasures like Litchfield Beach, Pawleys Island, DeBordieu, Brookgreen Gardens, Hobcaw Barony, the Tom Yawkey Wildlife Center, Murrells Inlet and, best of all, the town of Georgetown. This book is for Georgetown.

ACKNOWLEDGEMENTS

When I was researching the material for this book, it was common to ask a man if he knew anything about the Sunset Lodge in Georgetown and for him to hold up his hand and say, "Well, I never went there but let me tell you a story." Most men had not, in fact, ever been to the brothel, and those few who had and who told me about their visit had and still have a strong interest in not being identified. For some men, it's an embarrassing experience to admit to having had, although I will say some guys were all about it and gave me far more detail than I wanted to hear.

I talked to business owners, the sons and daughters of business owners, local professionals, residents of Georgetown, out-of-towners who hunted and fished in Georgetown and many, many more. Once I had written a rough manuscript, a group of folks read my narratives and offered grammatical as well as structural advice. I then rewrote and rewrote and rewrote. A friend told me if an author does not hate his book by the time he publishes it, then he did not spend enough time writing and rewriting it. I will say I have worked up a strong dislike for *Sunset Lodge in Georgetown: The Story of a Madam*.

Here is the list of people I want to thank for helping me. Some of these folks will read this list and wonder how or why they are on the list. They are on the list because they helped me, either by telling me stories, encouraging me or providing me information I could use. Most authors write in solitude; I have written this book almost publicly. Friends have asked me for years how my book is coming along, and some have asked, "Are you ever going to finish that book?"

To those friends who are not acknowledged in these pages, I am sorry; or, depending on how you feel about being named in a book about a brothel, you're welcome. Some may say *Whew* when they do not find their names.

There are two individuals who helped me write this book:

Paige Sawyer set up meetings for me, interviewed folks I could not get to Georgetown to see, read and reread my manuscripts and prepared the pictures for this book. Paige is a professional photographer in Georgetown. He was my researcher, my sounding board, my idea man, my encourager and my very good friend. This book literally could not have happened without Paige.

Bob Hodges is my brother. He is a retired judge on the Federal Claims Court. He and I have been e-mailing since the use of e-mails became understandable by old guys like us. We have told secrets, sorted through personal problems together, written long screeds, expressed opinions and entertained each other by e-mail. My early narratives were written in the form of e-mails to Bob. He seemed to enjoy reading my stories, and he encouraged me to write this book. Bob is the inspiration that kept me writing.

During my information accumulation stage, I entertained my wife, Susan Graybill Hodges, during wine-drinking time at home with stories I had heard, and she was an appreciative audience. I did not think there was a way I could write a book the way I thought a book needed to be written. I embarrass easily, and the material was challenging. I piddled around a few years, and finally Sue said, "Write the book!" Sue is a patient woman, and I am sure I have tested the limits of her patience. Thank you, Sue, for your support and your encouragement.

A storytelling book relies on the strength of the stories one hears, and I hit the jackpot when I found Tammy Foxworth. Tammy's parents, Jack and Bettye Marsh, bought the Sunset Lodge building from Hazel Weisse in late 1969–early 1970, when Tammy was a child. Tammy asked her mom to meet with me one day in Jack Scoville's conference room, and I had three entertaining hours trading stories with Bettye. She gave me documents and artifacts, and she shared her memories. At the end of our visit, Bettye said, "Well, David, you have had sex explained to you by a seventy-nine-year-old lady!"

There were two men who each talked to me privately to tell me stories that I simply would not have believed otherwise. You cannot make up this stuff! Thank you to both of them for trusting me with their stories.

I appreciate Paige Sawyer, Bob Hodges, Sue Hodges, Tammy Foxworth, Joan Stewart, Lee Brockington, Charles Swenson, Val Littlefield, Pat Ferris,

Acknowledgements

Ralph Ford Jr., Jeep Ford, George Geer, Doc Lachicotte, Diane Seale, John Napier, Gerti Dorn, Nelson Chandler, Nick Zeigler, Dorn Smith, Jack Graybill, Nick and KK Nicholson, Jennifer Walker, Jack Hodges, John Jenrette, Brendon Barber, Jack Scoville, Vince Weaver, Bettye Marsh, Edna Knox, Doug McClary, Dwight McInvaill, Lep Boyd, Georgia Cooper, Vivian Richburg, Woody Gruber, Nat and Marcia Kaminski, Bob Lumpkin, Cathy Lumpkin, Mike McDonald, Dewey Ervin, Mike Schwartz, Graham Osteen, Ted Quantz, Bobby Roberts, Julie Warren, Phil Wilkinson, Phil Wilson, Dick Stanland, Allen Stokes, Randy Dunlap, Pledger Lawton, Gerry Kenyon, Jeepy Ford, Alex Miller, Barry Price, Rusty Hammond, Bill Doar, Jim Morton, Tommy Pope, Raad Joseph, Margaret Kinard, Steve Williams, Mick Lindsay, Leah Gore, Dave Rowe, Mary Jane Reynolds, Stan Ingram, Lib McElveen, Charlie Schooler, Pat Schooler, Derek Thomas, Anne Martin, Roger Blackman, Ashley Carter, Patti Burns, Wallace Cottingham, Charles Moore, Chip Daniels, Ross Holmes, Dino Thompson, Helen Milliken, Trudy Bazemore, Bucky Watkins, Egerton Burroughs, Ann Gibbes, Jason Lesley, Cal McMeekin, Paul Joseph, Debbie Avinger, Charles Ragsdale, Virginia Skinner, Suzanne Linder, Becky Godwin, Billy Jenkinson, Faye Pender and, finally, Dave Howser, who asked me every time I saw him if I would be finishing this book during his lifetime.

THE HISTORY

GEORGETOWN COUNTY, SOUTH CAROLINA

Georgetown, South Carolina, in 1940 was a small southern town with a remarkable amount of influence from outside the county. Unlike most towns, Georgetown was a destination for wealthy men. Why? Ducks! The Atlantic Flyway was a major migration route for ducks that followed the coast of Greenland along the Eastern Shore to the Gulf of Mexico, and ducks loved the rice fields in Georgetown County.

In recent years, the Flyway has become less significant as duck habitats have been destroyed and property developed, but during the late 1800s, hunters reported the sky black with ducks. Pictures of hunters crouched in front of or behind massive piles of ducks were common. President Grover Cleveland and his friends shot 401 ducks in one day.[8] In Neal Cox's very fine memoir, he discussed the old rice fields at Arcadia Plantation that "were alive with thousands of wild ducks circling in every direction. There were mallards, black ducks, teal, scaup, wood ducks, and other species that I had never seen before."[9]

Before the Civil War, in 1840, Georgetown County was the richest county in the United States because of rice grown along the five rivers that flow into Winyah Bay and the Atlantic Ocean. The county grew as much as half the rice grown in the United States.[10]

The plantation owners along the rivers were massively wealthy. Plowden Weston was a major rice producer, as was his father. Weston lived on Hagley Plantation at Pawleys and lived well on the interest earned on roughly $1 million in assets.[11] There were forty rice plantations on the Waccamaw

River, fifty on the Pee Dee and Black River and another fifty-four in the Santee River Delta.[12]

Growing rice and enslaving people went hand in hand. Plantation owners planted thousands of acres of rice, and to prepare the land, enslaved people had to clear the large white gum, cedar and cypress trees and to build banks around the land to hold the water. The mud was so soft that a worker had to step from one root to another to avoid sinking. The undergrowth was dense and difficult to pass through without briars tearing flesh and clothing.[13] This effort took manual labor and lots of it. In 1860, the population of Georgetown County was 85 percent black, the highest percentage of enslaved persons to the total population in any county this side of the Mississippi.[14]

The American Civil War started in the Charleston, South Carolina harbor in 1860. In 1865, General Sherman's Union troops marched from Savannah, Georgia, through the center of South Carolina and into North Carolina burning homes and eating crops and stealing silver. They stole barnyard animals for food, often leaving South Carolinians with nothing to eat. The white people and the black people of South Carolina suffered through the Civil War and suffered again through the Reconstruction era. The people of South Carolina were bitter and resentful of northerners for a long, long time.

After the Civil War, there were no enslaved people. Plantation owners like Elizabeth W. Allston Pringle (Patience Pennington) tried to compensate the newly freed workers to continue to plant the rice, dig the weeds, repair the banks, clear obstructions in the rice trunks (that easily could be an alligator) and manage the growing process. She split the income with her employees, but it was a difficult business, and she was struggling.[15] The hurricane of 1893 stayed in Georgetown two days with winds reaching 120 miles per hour. Six weeks later, another hurricane arrived and did yet more damage to the rice fields. Hurricanes in the 1890s destroyed the banks and flooded the fields with salt water that the owners of the land could not afford to repair. Also, the market for rice was moving away from South Carolina. By 1900, New Orleans had replaced Georgetown as the center of the rice industry in the United States. Rice production had become mechanized with heavy steam-powered machinery, but the soft mud of South Carolina rice fields could not hold the heavy machines.[16] The rice plantation owners began to sell their property to men who had enough money to maintain the fields and who wanted to hunt ducks.

Only forty years after General Sherman burned a path through South Carolina, rich northern men invaded Georgetown County early in the

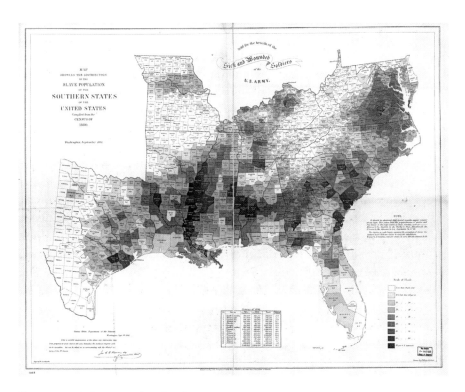

County population map of enslaved persons.

twentieth century, using weapons of cash instead of guns, buying the property their fathers and grandfathers took by force. This time, the northerners were welcomed by most citizens of the area. Local businesses benefited from absentee northern plantation owners who relied on Front Street businessmen to pay their employees, sell them supplies and provide them Lowcountry planting expertise.[17]

To grow rice, plantation owners took advantage of ocean tides pushing water up the rivers. Salt water flowing upriver from the ocean is heavier than fresh water flowing down the river. The "salt point" is the place upriver that has enough fresh water to create a three-foot "liquid wedge" on top of the salty ocean water.[18] By using rice trunks built into the banks, the owners could flood the rice fields at high tide with fresh water and, when it was time to dry out the rice plants, reverse the flow and drain the fields at low tide.

Duck hunters look for shallow ponds, less than two feet deep, to attract some types of ducks. Existing rice fields were ideal for duck hunting because the fields already had been cleared, banks already had been built and the rice trunks already had been installed. The new plantation owners continued to plant rice but left some of the crop in the field. When ducks migrated south on the Atlantic Flyway, the old rice plantations were an attractive place to stop, just as ducks had been doing for hundreds of years.

When President Grover Cleveland arrived in Georgetown County in 1894, he managed to get his 265-pound frame stuck in the mud while hunting ducks. His guide saved him by wrapping his arms around the president and pulling him out of the pluff mud. "The President's boots stayed where they were." His misadventure made the national newspapers, and rich men in the North discovered duck hunting in South Carolina.[19]

In 1905, native South Carolinian Bernard Baruch returned to Georgetown from making his fortune on Wall Street. Baruch grew up in Camden. When he was eleven years old, his family moved to New York, where he graduated from City College. He then became a stockbroker and became wealthy, making $1 million in the late 1800s. He bought a seat on the New York Stock Exchange before turning thirty years old. He later became a national defense advisor to Woodrow Wilson and then a policy advisor to Franklin Roosevelt and later to Harry Truman.[20] A newspaper article in 1912 referred to Bernard Baruch as a daring speculator who had just made $20 million on one transaction in the stock market.[21]

Bernard Baruch bought multiple plantations in Georgetown County, totaling sixteen thousand acres, now called Hobcaw Barony. He invited his friends from New York to hunt in Georgetown, and they, in turn, looked for plantations to buy for themselves. The men following Bernard Baruch in buying plantations included I.E. Emerson, A.M. Huntington, Jesse Metcalf, D.L. Pickman, Edwin G. Siebels, Bill Yawkey and Eugene DuPont. By World War II, over one hundred plantations in Georgetown County were owned by northerners.[22]

One of the rich northern men who was inspired by Bernard Baruch to buy plantations in Georgetown County was Bill Yawkey, the son of the richest man in Michigan. While people in the North and the South were fighting one another and burning one another's homes during the Civil War, men like Bill Yawkey's father were making a fortune in mining and lumber. When Bill Yawkey died in 1919, he left the family fortune, including his share of several South Carolina plantations, to his nephew Tom Yawkey. In 1925, Tom bought the other shares until he owned all of North Island and South Island and half of Cat Island, located just south of the town of Georgetown.[23] Just four days after Tom Yawkey was given access to his trust account at age thirty in 1933, he bought the Boston Red Sox baseball team and Fenway Park in Boston.[24] He lived in Boston during the baseball season and spent his winters in Georgetown. Tom Yawkey owned the Red Sox and his Georgetown property for the rest of his life. He died in 1976.

Local real estate brokers and lawyers started the Carolina Plantation Society in 1935 to encourage plantation owners to invite their friends to join them in South Carolina.[25] George Rogers, in his *History of Georgetown County*, describes the creation of the Carolina Plantation Society. Rogers expresses his opinion that without those plantation owners, Georgetown County might not have survived the Depression. The northerners spent extra money in Georgetown County during the Depression to help soften the financial blow to the local population. They hired staff to plant food plots for animals. They provided jobs and built new homes for themselves and "far more brick walls than any home needed."[26] They built homes on their property for their black employees to live in and churches in which they could worship. They even provided free medical clinics to care for their employees and families.

The *Georgetown Times* published its newspaper on Friday, October 16, 1936, with the headline announcing the "Largest Paper Mill in World to Be Erected." The article said Georgetown was chosen for the $8 million plant, and the expectation was that the plant would be in operation by October 1, 1937. Workmen began clearing the five-hundred-acre site immediately.[27]

On the same day the construction project was announced, an editorial in the *Georgetown Times* chided the people of Georgetown for trying to profit at the expense of the newcomers to town. The editorial accused the citizens of having contracted the disease of "dollar madness" as rooms in homes and apartments and houses were priced sky-high to accommodate the new workers at the plant.[28]

Clarence Phillips was a realtor in Georgetown County who created a map that was used in the North to advertise the properties along the rivers that already were owned by northerners. Of thirty-four properties listed on the map, at least eighteen owners were from New York State, and the heading of the map read, "They know the whole world, and this is their playground." Phillips put notices in *Field and Stream* magazine to advertise properties for sale in South Carolina. One advertisement in the October 1922 issue said, "900 acres, four miles from railroad station. Excellent Deer, Turkey, Quail and Duck Shooting. Seven-room dwelling, good land, some timber, good fishing, property fronts on Sampit River. All of the above for $10,000. Write or wire Clarence C. Phillips, Georgetown, S.C."[29]

As airplanes became more popular and considered safe to fly, some of the plantation owners built grass runways on their property and bought planes to carry them from New York to Georgetown. Walker Inman bought one of the first corporate airplanes built after World War II, the Lockheed Electra. Belle Baruch bought a single-engine Stinson and a twin-engine Beechcraft.[30] The ease with which visitors could enter and leave Georgetown County created more opportunity for residents to have contact with people who lived in other parts of the country.

Another source of outside influence in Georgetown came from the water. Georgetown is located on the Intracoastal Waterway, the water highway for commercial shipping and pleasure boating. Early in our history, the federal government explored the possibility of creating an inland route for shipping without having to travel on the open sea. Most of the route already existed with rivers and natural inlets, but there were significant sections that were not connected. Over a period of one hundred years, Congress periodically appropriated funds to complete the Intracoastal Waterway, and the final construction of the Eastern Seaboard Intracoastal Waterway was finished in the late 1930s.

The Intracoastal Waterway had an impact on the people in Georgetown. The people who visited Georgetown on boats and yachts paid to dock for the night, they bought supplies and food on Front Street and they shopped in the stores. Marina employees tell of yachts that arrived in Georgetown piloted by their owners or by the owner's captain, as well as yachts bringing celebrities or even mafia bosses. Some men who arrived in Georgetown made their way to the Sunset Lodge, some stayed on their boats and others just restocked their boats and left. The folks on Front Street in Georgetown were used to seeing strangers in their stores, and the store inventories reflected the interests of a clientele broader than just the residents of Georgetown.

Georgetown is a port town. Over eight thousand people lived there in 1940. Transportation was improving; there were three major roads leading into town—Highways 17, 521 and 701—and all were paved. The Lafayette Bridge was completed in 1935, connecting Florida to Maine on Highway 17; it was called the Coastal Road and became the primary thoroughfare along the coast.

Shipping was a major source of income and influence for the county. Georgetown was connected to New York, Wilmington and Charleston by water. A four-masted schooner, *Annie C. Ross*, could travel from New York to Georgetown in five days.[31] Goods left Georgetown for ports worldwide. One store, C.L. Ford, on Front Street, bought inventory from schooners that delivered goods for sale.[32] Many residents reported they could not afford to buy the specialty products C.L. Ford had to sell. Ford offered everything from canned rattlesnake to caviar. It stocked wine, fresh chickens and the best cuts of beef and pork.[33] The plantation owners and the wealthier Georgetonians provided the store with a good business.

C.L. Ford opened in the mid-1890s. Charles Ford owned the store until his death in 1936, and his son Ralph owned the store until his death in 1958. Charles and Ralph actively developed relationships with the plantation owners and were able to serve as paymaster for the employees of some of the plantations. The black employees who went to C.L. Ford on Saturday payday would enter from the river side of the store, and the white patrons walked in from Front Street. The employees would buy supplies for themselves and generally leave for their plantation homes with more supplies than money.

The employees at International Paper generated enough income to help the store owners on Front Street justify buying better stock for inventory and to keep their stores fresher. The Georgetown stores were much more profitable in 1940 than during the Depression. There were grocery and hardware stores, flower shops, restaurants, pharmacies, furniture stores, department stores, lots of ladies' clothing stores, jewelry stores, optometrists, doctors, banks, cafés, dry cleaners, a couple of hotels and even a Western Auto.

For entertainment, they had the Palace Theatre, the Peerless and the Strand. They had the Whistling Pig by the Lafayette Bridge. Also, it was no secret the Sunset Lodge brothel was in town. The madam, Hazel Weisse, shopped on Front Street, openly donated to charitable causes and allowed her employees to shop on Front Street. When Georgetown residents are asked why they allowed a brothel to exist in the county for thirty-three years without a significant challenge, there is no answer. Hazel was discreet and she did not embarrass the town, and the residents let it go. The men did not talk about the Sunset Lodge, at least with the women. The Sunset Lodge was located three miles south of Front Street on the road to Charleston, and there was no sign in front of the house. Unlike many brothels, Hazel did not allow her employees to speak to men on Front Street or loiter on the corners. It was easy to leave her be.

The Georgetown residents coped with Hazel's presence in town by accommodating the traffic and confusion she caused. Many residents routinely gave visiting men directions to the Sunset Lodge. One man said his ten-year-old son did not know what the Sunset Lodge was, but he could give excellent directions.

Were the people in Georgetown more accepting of the Sunset Lodge because of outside influences on the town? Unlike towns in the interior,

Georgetown had a more sophisticated population, and unlike Georgetown, Charleston and Beaufort had military bases that disrupted residents with visiting soldiers. The northerners who owned plantations in Georgetown County brought money to town and a more stable attitude; perhaps they were a bit older too. The visitors who arrived by boat or yacht on the Intracoastal Waterway brought money, and the merchants on Front Street stocked their shelves with merchandise for the visitors. Hazel Weisse could not have chosen a better place to open the type of business she owned with her specific business model of a single location, no solicitation and perhaps a higher behavior and appearance requirement for her customers.

HAZEL WEISSE

(1900–1974)

Hazel Weisse arrived in Georgetown in 1936, set up a brothel, ran it openly for thirty-three years and retired on her terms. When residents in Georgetown have told stories about Hazel and her brothel, it hardly ever has been with disapproval. There were a few critical comments, but for the most part, Hazel was accepted in Georgetown as a member of the community. Her philanthropic behavior led one woman to comment, "Hazel was our own United Way."

Born in 1900 in Paoli, Orange County, Indiana, a town of 1,200, Hazel lived with her dad and her older sister after her mom died. Hazel graduated from Paoli High School in 1916. The family moved to Indianapolis, where her dad worked as a conductor for the Indianapolis street railroad system. Hazel got pregnant and delivered a baby in 1919 in Indianapolis. The baby's father was listed on the birth certificate as a laborer, and Hazel was a teacher. She was nineteen and he was twenty-three years old. Hazel and the baby's father were not married, so the child was given Hazel's maiden name.

By 1920, Hazel had moved from Indiana to Illinois and was living in Ward 14, Cook County, Chicago. She lived in a boardinghouse and worked as a stenographer in the Butter Press Industry. The production and sale of alcoholic products was outlawed by the United States Constitution in 1920, and a period of prohibition began in America. Organized crime in large cities thrived, and Chicago became known for speakeasies, gangsters and prostitution. One gangster was said to have owned over two hundred brothels in Chicago in 1920. The city was violent as competing gangs protected

Hazel Weisse at Christmas. *Courtesy of Tammy Marsh Foxworth.*

their territory and settled scores. There are no references to Hazel's time in Chicago. One assumes she became a prostitute in Chicago if she wasn't already because she later moved from Chicago to Florence, South Carolina, and opened a brothel.

Hazel married once. The lucky guy was John Weisse, a bartender. He was granted a divorce from Hazel in October 1928 in Muncie, Indiana. John Weisse testified that Hazel possessed a high temper and frequently cursed him, and she did not take care of him.[31] The marriage ended quickly but lasted long enough for Hazel to take his name and keep it for the rest of her life, thereby cloaking her son in anonymity.

Hazel's son changed his last name from Hazel's maiden name to his birth dad's last name. He later worked for a large corporation in Indiana. In 1949, when he was thirty years old, he bought a house on Folly Beach in South

Carolina next door to a house that his mom owned. Hazel then bought a second house at Folly Beach and kept them both until 1968, the year before she retired from her brothel. Hazel and her son then sold the houses. Hazel sold her houses to different buyers, and her son sold his house to Hazel for "$5 and love and affection."

Stories are told about how Hazel's son did not know what she did for a living and how she would meet him in Charleston instead of Georgetown to protect him from the truth. Well, the truth is he had to know about Hazel's business. Even though the Folly Beach houses were not used for Hazel's prostitution activities, she used the houses as a rest retreat for the women working for her. When Hazel was in her final illness in 1974, her son and his wife arrived in Georgetown to sort through Hazel's jewelry and the safe deposit box.[35] Hazel ultimately left her sizable estate to her son and to her grandchildren in Indiana.

Hazel left Chicago and moved to Florence, South Carolina, before 1930. Why did she leave Chicago and why did she choose to move to Florence? Did she know someone in Florence she wanted to be near? Was she running from someone in Chicago, or perhaps did someone in Chicago send her to Florence? Every town of any size across this country in the 1920s had brothels that Hazel could have joined, or she could have started her own brothel. Why Florence?

Florence had more than its share of brothels in the late 1930s. The Florence train station was the busiest in South Carolina with fourteen passenger trains each day.[36] Hazel owned property on Commander Street, just a few blocks from the train station. There is no trace of Hazel in Florence other than entries in the Florence City Directory and the newspaper reference to the sale of her property on Commander Street in 1939, three years after she left Florence, to Jessie Barnwell.[37] Hazel did not become part of the Florence community as she did in Georgetown. There are no published charitable contributions in Florence, and her stay in Florence was so long ago—eighty-three years—that there are no stories about Hazel in Florence as there still are in Georgetown. Also, Hazel was in her twenties and early thirties in Florence. She was not yet the businessperson she would become.

Hazel lived in Florence from 1928 until 1936. The 1930 federal census lists her occupation as boardinghouse owner with three boarders living in the house, all single women under twenty-five years old. Hazel was in a convenient location in Florence and she had her business where she wanted it, but her days in Florence were numbered.

The chief of police in the town of Florence had held that position for fourteen years, and the mayor of the town of Florence had been serving for twenty-five years. Dexter Ernest Ellerbe ran for mayor of Florence in 1935 on the platform of firing the chief of police for failing to shut down the houses of prostitution. Ellerbe won that race. At the first city council meeting after the election, he led a successful effort to oust the chief of police along with three other police department employees.[38] No doubt, Hazel felt unwelcome.

It is easy to explain why Hazel moved from Florence to Georgetown. The Depression in America had been raging for years, banks were closed and railroads had stopped running. Everyone felt the impact of low employment and tight conditions. In 1936, Georgetown County received the very good news of the immediate construction of International Paper's newest paper mill, the largest paper and pulp mill in the world.[39] The arrival of International Paper was an economic lifesaver for the county.

Hazel bought a house three miles south of Georgetown in August 1936, two months before the public announcement of the construction of the paper mill. The road she settled on was the Coastal Road, a highway completed in 1935 that connected Florida with Maine. Her new brothel was not on a train line as in Florence but was on the major highway between Georgetown and Charleston that connected Hazel with potential customers up and down the East Coast. She accurately interpreted the changes happening in the transportation system in America.

Hazel's new house was on five acres and previously had belonged to a well-known bootlegger. Hazel paid $2,700 for the house, which represented about 90 percent of her annual income. How did she afford to buy her new house? She did not sell her Florence house until three years later to Jessie Barnwell. The story is that Tom Yawkey, the owner of the Boston Red Sox baseball team and of twenty thousand acres of hunting property in Georgetown, lent Hazel the money to buy the house.

When Hazel arrived in Georgetown, the only airport was a grass runway on Merriman Road. During World War II, the United States Army Air Force built an airport with concrete runways directly across the Coastal Road from Hazel's brothel. After the war, the federal government deeded the airport property to Georgetown County, and Hazel had convenient access by air to the rest of the Southeast and even to New York. Men could now fly into the airport, get a ride across the highway to the Sunset Lodge and be on their way home in time for dinner. One high school student reported receiving a fifty-dollar tip for driving a man across the highway to the brothel and back to his plane. Hazel also used the airport to bring in women who would stay a season before flying to another brothel or back home.

The Intracoastal Waterway was the other major access into Georgetown that benefited Hazel. Boats, ships and yachts entered Georgetown waters from ports as far south as Key West and as far north as Boston without having to venture into the open seas. The Intracoastal Waterway was largely completed by 1936 when Hazel arrived in Georgetown. The South Carolina section of the Intracoastal Waterway was over two hundred miles long and was dredged over nine feet deep. The marina on Front Street competed with other ports. Georgetown marina personnel have acknowledged that the presence of the Sunset Lodge gave the men on the boats a reason to choose the marina at Georgetown over nearby marinas.

Hazel moved into her new building and was open for business. She named her business Sunset Lodge for unknown reasons. Most brothels used the name of the madam as the name of the brothel, such as Ann's or Ruby's in Florence, but Hazel chose Sunset Lodge.

The Sunset Lodge was a two-story house with four bedrooms upstairs and one bathroom. The downstairs had a kitchen, dining room, living room, bathroom and front hall. She kept the front door and the back door locked. Customers parked in the back of the house and rang the back doorbell to be let in. There were three brick steps that led from the back yard into the house. By the time the Sunset Lodge closed in 1969, the bricks were worn down by the tens of thousands of shoes that had slid across the steps.

The driveway at the Sunset Lodge was circular around the back of the house with an entrance to the road on either side of the building. Customers would turn into the driveway where a wagon wheel was displayed and park in the back. There was no sign, and men got confused. Hazel's next-door neighbor posted a sign in her front yard that said, "This isn't it!" Customers sensitive about their cars being visible would hide them in the woods in the back of Hazel's property or would park in a restaurant parking lot and hire a cab to take them to the Sunset Lodge. The cab drivers would charge extra for the trip because the Sunset Lodge was outside town limits. There are many stories of the marina manager in Georgetown, the bellman from the Ocean Forest Hotel in Myrtle Beach, friends or even dads sitting downstairs at the dining room table while customers were upstairs.

Hazel charged three dollars in 1936 when she opened her brothel in Georgetown. Hazel increased the fee from three dollars in 1936 to twenty dollars by the time the Sunset Lodge closed in 1969. Who had three dollars in 1936? Was the market large enough for Hazel to generate much revenue? How did Hazel find men who had enough available funds in their entertainment budget to spend it at the Sunset Lodge?

Margaret Mitchell's book *Gone with the Wind*[10] also was published in 1936 and was criticized for costing so much; the book cost three dollars. The book sold 176,000 copies in 1936, and by 1938, it had sold over 1 million copies. There were plenty of men who would have chosen a Sunset Lodge experience over owning a copy of *Gone with the Wind*.

Hazel was the victim of many practical jokes. She walked her property every morning to move the signs left overnight by high school students. It was common to see signs saying *For Rent* or *We Give Green Stamps* or *Men and Equipment Working*. Riding around the back of the Sunset Lodge was a common evening activity for young drivers. Carloads of girls left their Methodist Youth Fellowship (MYF) meetings and drove around the back of the Sunset Lodge, blew the horn and yelled out the window and then talked about their experiences all the way back to the safety of their neighborhoods. One group of girls drove around the Sunset Lodge, and one girl jumped on another and tickled her and pushed her down so she would not see her father's car parked behind the building.

The inside of the Sunset Lodge was set up for men to relax in the living room on two long sofas. Hazel put a jukebox in the living room for men to play songs and to dance with the sporting ladies. She sold beer and liquor to the customers from a bar set up in the living room. One man complained about the one-dollar beer at a time when beer at the Whistling Pig cost a quarter, and Hazel said, "You did not come here to drink."

Hazel had a phone hidden behind the pantry curtain beside the kitchen. The phone had an unlisted number because she did not want wives calling the Sunset Lodge looking for their husbands. She had a handwritten phone list on the wall with the names and numbers of the vendors she needed to call. A nurse at the hospital had Hazel's phone number because a group of doctors and business owners often played poker in the living room at the Sunset Lodge, and she would call Hazel if there was an emergency at the hospital.

The poker games were casual and among friends. Hazel did not run a gambling house. The Sunset Lodge was not a Chicago-style speakeasy with gangster-style activities. She was single-minded. Her business model was sex. She sold a lot of liquor, and to keep the folks in Georgetown ignorant of just how much alcohol she served, she also bought liquor from a store in Myrtle Beach. There was a column in the October 6, 1966 *Georgetown Times* that had this paragraph: "A recent 'raid' in Georgetown saw tax agents call on the Moose Club and VFW but not visit a house of prostitution where liquor is sold too. Is this law enforcement? It strikes us more as being political harassment."[41] There was no criticism of the house of prostitution itself, just the inconsistent enforcement of the liquor law.

Hazel rightfully was criticized for allowing underage males in her building, but she did not allow them to drink alcohol and there was no gambling. She drew an odd line of acceptable behavior. One man gave his son fifty dollars on his eighteenth birthday to take to the Sunset Lodge. The money was burning a hole in his pocket. He looked around and announced he would buy everyone there a drink. Hazel pulled him aside and told him he could pick out a girl, even two or three girls, but he was not old enough to drink.

The women of the Sunset Lodge lived in upstairs bedrooms and in the trailers and pink cabin in the back. Hazel herself lived in a garage apartment behind the Sunset Lodge. Hazel had an intercom system in the Sunset Lodge that extended to the trailers and the cabin out back. The intercom also was hidden behind the curtain in the pantry. There were nine ports in the intercom. She had four bedrooms upstairs and, at the time of her closing, two two-bedroom trailers and the pink cabin. She had each bedroom wired so she could listen to make sure her girls were safe.

Residential air-conditioner sales expanded dramatically in the 1950s. When window air-conditioner units became available, Hazel bought enough units to cool the entire house. Her challenge was that her transformer was not large enough to handle the additional load. In 1959, Santee Electric Cooperative replaced her 15 KVA transformer with a 25 KVA transformer so Hazel would have sufficient power for her building.

When a man rang the back doorbell, Hazel would answer the door. She would determine if the man was dangerous, drunk or dirty. If she let him in, he would be told to sit in the living room. If he chose to dance or drink or just to visit, there was no pressure on him to choose a girl. If he chose a girl, he would pay the fee at the bottom of the steps before going upstairs. In the early days, an older lady would sit at a table with a cash box and take the money. Once upstairs, the girl would take over.

One woman was convinced her husband was in the Sunset Lodge, so she waited outside until a man walked in, and she then bolted through the open door. She ran through the downstairs calling his name and then ran upstairs and into the rooms. Her husband indeed was in one of the rooms, and he hid behind the door when his wife looked in.

Hazel owned and managed a big business. Prostitution is a big business. She generally had at least a half dozen women living there at any one time.

Even if each woman stayed one year, Hazel still had at least two hundred women working for her while she owned the Sunset Lodge. Hazel's women at the end of her career had not even been born when Hazel first arrived in Georgetown.

Hazel spent a lot of money in Georgetown County. She bought furniture, mattresses, cars, food every day, supplies, jewelry, clothes and shoes, and she had dry cleaning. She bought bonds at the bank and money orders at the post office. Her sporting ladies shopped on Front Street and bought whatever they saw that they wanted. They also mailed presents home in plain boxes with plain wrappers so their families would not know where they were living. Merchants on Front Street bought inventory with the women of the Sunset Lodge in mind. The stores in Georgetown had more stock, better stock and more trendy stock than other towns of similar size.

The "seventy-two-year rule" determines when personally identifying data gathered by federal census workers may be released to the public. Information about a specific person may not be released for seventy-two years. The most recent census that has been made available by the U.S. Census Bureau is from 1940. The 1950 census will be released in 2022.

In 1940, according to the census, Hazel Weisse was forty years old, divorced and owned a boardinghouse in Georgetown County with a five-member black family living on the property. When the census worker interviewed Hazel, three single women lived in the house, ages thirty-three, thirty and twenty-five. Her admitted income from the boardinghouse was $3,033, with no income from other sources.

Stairs at Sunset Lodge.
Courtesy of Tammy Marsh Foxworth.

So, how much was $3,033 in 1940? The 1940 federal wage or salary report for South Carolina shows there were 76,000 men and 26,000 women who had worked twelve months in 1939 in the category of Rural—Non Farm. Of those 76,000 men, only 1,400 made over $3,000. Of those 26,000 women, only 23 made over $3,000. Hazel had been in Georgetown fewer than five years and already was one of the highest-compensated women in South Carolina.

Hazel expressed her wealth by the purchase of a new car each year, by the conspicuous consumption of high-end clothes and shoes but mostly by her generosity toward the community. Hazel Weisse gave away a lot of money. Charitable contributions could have been her business model, but it was effective just the same.

Every Thanksgiving, Hazel paid for thirty food baskets to be distributed to families in need. She left it up to Ralph Ford, the owner of her favorite grocery store, the C.L. Ford store, to decide who would receive the baskets. She contributed to the March of Dimes, the Hospital Endowment Fund and Easter Seals, and the rumor is she gave money to help sponsor Little League baseball teams and even contributed to a church building fund. She was an easy ask for anyone raising money for charity.

Hazel silently gave money to families that had a fire or to families in which the father had died in a work accident. One black cab driver was in a car accident and was unable to drive. Hazel's chauffeur went to the man and handed him $300 and told him the money was from the community. One person said the women on an annual fundraising committee tried to get assigned to solicit Hazel each year because it was an automatic gift. The residents of Georgetown did not hesitate to engage Hazel in the needs of the community and freely requested her assistance. It was said Hazel tried to give away more money each year than did International Paper.

Hazel Weisse was an impressive businessperson. She controlled her business environment. Retired law enforcement personnel have said there was no trouble at the Sunset Lodge; Hazel took care of business. She also controlled the women who worked for her. She would not let them go into town by themselves, and when they did go to town, a cab took them or Hazel's chauffeur drove her car. She made them go to the doctor every week to be checked for disease, and she put the certificate of good health under the glass by each girl's bedside table. One customer said the certificate made a big difference to him; he felt safer.

The girls opened savings accounts at the bank in Georgetown when they arrived, and it makes sense that they would. Prostitution is a cash business, and the Sunset Lodge had a lot of cash in the building. By Monday morning, Hazel wanted those women to put their cash in the bank to reduce the possibility of the girls stealing from one another. A banker on Front Street said the women of the Sunset Lodge would come by to close their accounts when they left Georgetown and that they generally withdrew at least $8,000. The average annual income for workers in South Carolina in 1960 was $3,800.

A postal worker said the ladies from the Sunset Lodge often went to the post office to buy $100 money orders. They then mailed several at a time, probably to family members. The post office workers had Hazel's unlisted phone number and would call if there was a problem. He remembered one time several ladies were buying money orders, and after they left, a worker realized he was missing the money for one money order. He called Hazel, and she sent $100 to the post office by taxi and said she would collect her money from the woman.

There are many stories about rich and powerful men who frequented the Sunset Lodge, from governors to congressmen to United States senators. An old joke often told involved the low-numbered license tags that were seen at the nationally known brothel, not just from South Carolina but from as far away as Ohio. Hazel cultivated relationships with men who could help her if she got into trouble and with men who could hurt her if it suited their purposes. She was known to spend time in Columbia when the South Carolina legislature was in session. She is believed to have catered to the Georgetown plantation owners by providing them women when the men had hunting guests. There are many stories of Tom Yawkey's Boston Red Sox baseball players hunting and fishing on his property in Georgetown.

The South Carolina legislature informally adjourned for one week each spring so the legislators and state senators could go to Georgetown to the Sunset Lodge. Hazel closed the Sunset Lodge that week to all customers but legislators and judges. The lawmakers would go by a private club on their way out of town to pick up box lunches. There were not many restaurants between Columbia and Georgetown in the 1960s, and they did not want to be seen walking into a restaurant together.

Hazel Weisse had a birthday party for herself every October 25. Attendance was by invitation only. Men arrived from everywhere. Everything that day was free, from the liquor downstairs to the women upstairs. The local florist did a good business delivering flowers to the Sunset Lodge. A gay friend of Hazel's told a friend with great humor and enthusiasm about standing in the living room at Hazel's party one year when a man from his church walked in. The man later told Hazel's gay friend that he was the last man he expected to see in a cathouse.

Hazel was never arrested, even when the sheriff shut down the Sunset Lodge in 1969. She was in business in Georgetown County for thirty-three years. The only time her name was in the newspaper was when she contributed money to the March of Dimes or other charitable fundraising efforts. When she opened her brothel in 1936, it would not have taken much for the sheriff to padlock the door and arrest the occupants, but it did not happen. She was allowed to grow her business, to become stronger financially and politically and ultimately to become bulletproof.

One story about why Hazel chose Georgetown for her brothel is that Tom Yawkey knew her from Florence when he took the train from New York to Florence, stayed a few days and then took a car into Georgetown. The story goes she needed to leave Florence after the new mayor, D.E. Ellerbe, fired the chief of police and her friend Tom Yawkey encouraged her to move to Georgetown. If that is what happened, it also would explain why she was not shut down immediately by the county sheriff. Tom Yawkey would have had significant influence in Georgetown, and perhaps he protected Hazel.

There are various stories about why and how Hazel closed the Sunset Lodge. A lot had happened in America from the time Hazel opened the Sunset Lodge in 1936 until she closed it in 1969. From the presidency of Franklin Roosevelt to Richard Nixon. From sitting by a console radio listening to a fireside chat to watching Gomer Pyle on a color television set. From the airplane flights of Amelia Earhart to the moonwalk of Neil Armstrong.

A lot had changed with Hazel as well. She was thirty-six years old when she arrived in Georgetown, and by her sixty-ninth birthday, she was weary. She had turned over the management of her brothel to a longtime employee, but like most business owners who watch successors run their businesses, Hazel was not happy. She had heart disease and kidney disease, she was sick and tired and she was ready to retire. She had a heart attack a couple of years after retiring and died two years after that.

There were also changes in Georgetown from the 1930s until the 1960s. When Hazel arrived, the Sunset Lodge was three miles from town, but the town moved closer. In the late 1950s, the community of Maryville was annexed into Georgetown. Also, the late 1960s was a turbulent time in America with riots, wars and assassinations. Circumstances changed.

When Hazel sold the property in December 1969 to Bettye and Jack Marsh, she continued to live in her garage apartment with her friend and caregiver, a black lady who took care of Hazel during her illness. Hazel sold the house and property, retaining a life estate in the garage apartment so she could continue to live there for the rest of her life. The Marshes watched over Hazel, and their daughter said she remembers Hazel as being a nice lady. Hazel had medical problems in 1972 that caused her and her friend to move to Ashley House in Charleston, where she would be close to Roper Hospital. She and her caregiver wrote letters to the Marsh family about Hazel's health and expressed the hope that they could move home soon—home being the garage apartment—but Hazel never fully recovered.

Hazel provided for her caregiver in her will. When Hazel died in 1974, her estate was valued at $276,000, including real estate, securities and even life insurance. Her will set aside $100,000 of assets for her black friend to receive all earnings each year for her lifetime. At the lady's death in 2001, the corpus of the funds went to Hazel's grandchildren. There are rumors of how very rich Hazel was by the time she died. There is no way to determine how much of Hazel's estate was transferred before her death and therefore was not counted in probate,

Sunset Lodge Closed, Fades From View

Sunset Lodge, a unique Georgetown County institution of international renown, was closed Friday as one phase of a state crack-down on illicit activities.

The 36-year-old brothel closed its doors on order of the Sheriff's Office. No charges were filed. Notice was served; Sunset hostesses packed their bags and left.

Sheriff Woodrow Carter said it was closed "indefinitely".

Sunset was a paradox of society. It was tolerated or ignored by most. In a seaport community, it was above board and self-disciplined. It was the source of frequent contributions to many civic causes.

It existed despite the blue laws of government. The transition from a straight-laced to a permissive society ironically brought its downfall.

Rampant back-street vice in other South Carolina cities and demands for uniform enforcement of law placed a spot light locally.

In a twist of fate, Sunset was eclipsed in the back-lash of a libertine age.

THE GEORGETOWN TIMES, Georgetown, S. C. December 18, 1969

Georgetown Times.

but an estate value of $276,000 in 1974, adjusted for inflation, would be worth about $1,500,000 today.

There were articles about the closing of the Sunset Lodge in the Georgetown newspaper, the Charleston newspapers and the Columbia newspaper. The heading of the Georgetown article was "Sunset Lodge Closed, Fades from View."[12] A Charleston article heading said, "Sunset Lodge Closed by County Sheriff."[13] Another article in Charleston said, "Sun Sets on Sunset Lodge,"[14] and the Columbia article said, "Sheriff Closes Sunset Lodge."[15] A follow-up article in the *State* paper two years later said, "Georgetown House Closed."[16]

CHARLESTON NEWS & COURIER Dec. 14, 1969
Sunset Lodge Closed By County Sheriff

GEORGETOWN — Georgetown County Sheriff Woodrow Carter said yesterday that he had closed an establishment south of Georgetown known as Sunset Lodge.

Carter identified it as a "widely-known house of prostitution," which he said has been operating in Georgetown County "since the early 1930s."

Carter said he closed the establishment "on my own," after receiving complaints on it "from county residents and all over the state. I think it's been operating out there long enough."

"It's closed indefinitely— as long as I'm sheriff," Carter added.

"It went out of operation Friday in the afternoon," Sheriff Carter told The News and Courier. "I just went out there and told the proprietor that they'd have to close it up."

"I talked to the proprietor, and she was very cooperative," he continued. "She did just what I asked her to and closed it up. There weren't any charges filed.

"If she'd refused to close it I would have had to go to court and get a court order to close," he said. "But she was most cooperative and sent all the girls away. There are no girls out there now," Carter said.

The sheriff said that operating a house of prostitution is a "violation of the law in Georgetown County and the state of South Carolina."

He said Sunset Lodge is located "about a mile on Highway 17 south of the (Georgetown) city limits.

"People know it from New York all over the United States and probably the whole world," Sheriff Carter said.

News and Courier.

The sheriff was quoted in a newspaper article as saying Hazel went to him and asked him to shut her down. It is likely the sheriff and Hazel had more than one conversation about closing the Sunset Lodge. They had known each other many years, and it is probable the sheriff used his personal influence and the power of his office to ease Hazel out of business. It is easy imagining him going to Hazel and saying, "It is time." A quiet closing without screaming police cars with flashing lights may not have been as satisfying to those who were past ready for Hazel to be arrested, but the sheriff was an effective force in Georgetown who accomplished much with his professional people skills.

The sheriff showed up on a Friday afternoon in mid-December 1969 and told everyone to leave. The women put their clothes in drawers and left. Bettye Marsh, the new owner of the property, said most of the chests of drawers were missing their drawers; however, the drawers found their way back to the house over the next year as women dropped them off or sent them by friends.

Hazel's health deteriorated in Charleston. One nurse who knew Hazel in Georgetown moved to Charleston and lived in the same building as Hazel. She waited at the elevator one day, and the doors opened to show a person on a stretcher with two attendants. She stepped onto the elevator but did not look at the person. She heard her name; it was Hazel on the stretcher.

Bettye and Jack Marsh drove to Charleston one day to visit with Hazel. Hazel begged Jack to put her in the bed of his truck and drive her back to the Sunset Lodge, but he said, "Hazel, I cannot do that."

Two months before Hazel's death, her power of attorney, who also was her stockbroker and friend, moved her to a nursing home in Indianapolis, where she died on July 15, 1974. Her obituary said she was a member of a local Methodist church. She is buried in Forest Lawn Cemetery in Indianapolis.

Hazel Weisse's death certificate listed her occupation as Retired—Investments.

THOMAS AUSTIN YAWKEY

(1903–1976)

Tom Yawkey's name continues to come up in connection with the Sunset Lodge. He was one of the richest men in America during the Depression. He owned the Boston Red Sox baseball team and Fenway Park. He also owned thousands of acres of old rice plantations in Georgetown, South Carolina.

Some people incorrectly believe Tom Yawkey owned the Sunset Lodge brothel. Others incorrectly believe he recruited Hazel Weisse to Georgetown at the behest of the city fathers to keep the Pittsburgh steelworkers busy while they were building the International Paper Mill. Still others incorrectly say Yawkey invited the Boston Red Sox baseball team to Georgetown each year on their way to spring training in Florida.

Tom Yawkey made his money the old-fashioned way: he inherited it. His asset accumulation was helped by his grandfather and his father dying the year Tom was born. Tom's mother died when he was fifteen years old and his uncle Bill died when he was sixteen, pretty much clearing the deck for Tom to inherit the entire Yawkey fortune.

Tom's grandfather was William Yawkey. Mr. Yawkey left his son Bill $10 million when he died in 1903, and he left his daughter Augusta, young Tom's mother, a sizable inheritance as well. Augusta died in 1918 of the flu during the pandemic, and she left her fifteen-year-old son Tom $4 million. Tom then inherited $20 million when his uncle Bill died of pneumonia in 1919. Tom received $500,000 in cash from uncle Bill, with the balance locked in a trust that he would be eligible to have when he turned thirty years old in 1933.[17]

Tom Yawkey's grandfather made a fortune in Michigan in mining and lumber. While people in the North and the South were killing one another during the Civil War and burning each other's homes, men like William Yawkey were making money. His two children, Bill and Augusta, lived large and died young, Bill at age forty-four and Augusta at age forty-seven.

Tom Yawkey did not start life as a Yawkey; his birth name was Austin. His mom, Augusta, married Tom Austin and had two children, Emma Marie in 1894 and Tom Austin Jr. in 1903. A few years after her husband died, Augusta turned over Emma Marie and Tom Jr. to her brother Bill Yawkey to raise. The children grew up in a luxury building alongside Central Park with cooks, maids and housekeepers. In 1910, Bill Yawkey married Margaret Draper, who became the aunt by marriage to Tom Austin Jr. and Emma Marie.

Tom Yawkey Austin Jr. changed his name to Tom Austin Yawkey when his uncle Bill adopted Tom in 1918 after Tom's mom died. Margaret Draper Yawkey then became Tom Yawkey's stepmother, and they appear to have been close and comfortable with each other.

The *New York Times* ran an article on March 18, 1919, headlined, "Schoolboy of 16 Inherits $20,000,000"[18] and referred to Tom Yawkey as one of the wealthiest boys in the country. Stepmom Margaret reportedly sat down her teenage stepson in front of four saucers. On three saucers were piles of beans representing the wealth of the Rockefellers, the Vanderbilts and the J.P. Morgans. On the fourth saucer, Margaret put one bean to represent the Yawkey money.[19]

For several years beginning in 1905, South Carolinian Bernard Baruch purchased and consolidated fourteen contiguous plantations in Georgetown County to use as a winter hunting preserve. The property stretched from the Atlantic Ocean to Winyah Bay. He named the sixteen-thousand-acre tract Hobcaw Barony. He invited his rich northern friends to South Carolina to hunt ducks, which caused owning Carolina plantations to become popular in the North. Bill Yawkey followed Baruch's lead by buying into a hunt club in Georgetown. By the Depression, few of the more than one hundred plantations along the five rivers that dump water into Winyah Bay and the Atlantic Ocean belonged to South Carolinians.

Bill Yawkey and his nephew Tom Austin, later Tom Yawkey, often went to South Carolina to hunt and fish at South Island, where Tom learned to love the land. After Bill died in 1919, Tom Yawkey inherited Bill's share of the hunt club on South Island,[50] and he became the sole owner by 1925 after buying out the other owners.[51]

Also in 1925, Tom Yawkey married Elise Sparrow, who had participated in the Miss America pageant in 1922 representing Birmingham, Alabama. He loved his property and he loved Elise, but he spent most of his time hunting and fishing in South Carolina, while Elise preferred the bright lights of New York. In 1936, they adopted a daughter who grew up with her mother. Tom Yawkey and his daughter did not have a close relationship. When asked later by reporters about her dad, she replied, "He is a strange man."[52]

Tom turned thirty in 1933 in the teeth of the Depression. His trust dissolved, and he had full access to the family fortune; four days later, he bought the Boston Red Sox baseball team, and he owned it for the rest of his life. He died in 1976.

Tom and Elise separated in 1939 and divorced in 1944. The story is that Tom first saw Jean Hiller, his second wife, while shopping with Elise at Jay Thorpe, an upscale dress shop in New York.[53] Jean modeled clothes for Elise to consider buying, and she caught Tom's eye. Jean moved in with Tom when Tom and Elise separated, and they lived together until Tom's divorce was final in 1944. Tom waited until Elise remarried in 1944 before marrying Jean.[54]

Tom's best friend in Georgetown was Ralph Ford, the owner of the C.L. Ford store on Front Street. Ralph was the first person Tom Yawkey called whenever he arrived in Georgetown. They hunted, fished and drank whiskey together. Tom went to the Ford home every week to see Ralph. Later, Jean ate lunch at the Ford home every Thursday.[55]

Ralph Ford Jr. used to tell the story of Tom and Jean getting married in his parents' home on Wood Street on Christmas Eve 1944. Ralph Jr. was fifteen years old. Ralph Jr. said his parents were so excited about the pending wedding that they painted the house, decorated extra-special for Christmas, put out their best china, cooked food and put on their best clothes for the event. Tom and Jean showed up for their wedding dressed in their hunting clothes; they had been out hunting. Ralph Jr. said the Yawkey casualness hurt his parents' feelings.[56]

Ralph Ford Sr.'s friendship with Tom Yawkey made it possible for him to ask Tom for a gift to help build a hospital in Georgetown. Tom and Jean were generous to charitable causes in Georgetown County. Of the northern rich men who owned plantations in Georgetown County, only Bernard Baruch, a native South Carolinian, was more generous.

Georgetown County only had one hospital until 1950, and it was started in 1925 by an African American woman, Florence Williams, who primarily served the black residents of Georgetown.[57] Residents with a dire medical need had to drive or be driven an hour north to Florence or an hour south to Charleston. The American Legion Post 114 in Georgetown decided to lead the effort to build a new hospital. Ralph Ford was the chairman of the steering committee. In 1945, he called Tom Yawkey one Sunday afternoon and asked to see him. Tom reminded Ralph they did not drink whiskey on Sundays, and Ralph agreed and drove to South Island. Tom was there, as was Tom's financial advisor, Frederick Defoe. Defoe was an attorney by training who became the secretary of the Boston Red Sox. He also was the executor of Tom Yawkey's uncle Bill's will.

Ralph explained the need for a hospital in Georgetown and the importance of a hospital to the town. He asked Tom if he would help pay for the hospital. Tom told Ralph his effort to build a hospital was noble and asked Ralph how much a hospital would cost. Ralph said $300,000.

"I'll give you that," Tom said.

Frederick Defoe said no, Tom could not give Ralph $300,000.

"Why not?" Tom asked.

Defoe told Tom he should give them $100,000 this year and another $100,000 each year for two more years. Tom asked Ralph if that would be okay, and Ralph said yes.

"Good, let's drink on it!" Tom said.[58]

The Georgetown newspaper on February 16, 1945, had a headline: "$100,000 Give to Hospital Fund."[59] The subheading said, "Wealthy Winter Resident Makes Large Donation." The article announced in the first sentence that "Thomas A. Yawkey, prominent Georgetown winter resident and owner of the Boston Red Sox baseball team, has made a $100,000 contribution to the Georgetown County Hospital Fund." The capital campaign continued to get everyone's buy-in and even finished the campaign with schoolchildren putting nickels and dimes in slots in cardboard sheets, but the real money was raised on that Sunday afternoon on South Island.

If you ask old men in Georgetown if they knew Tom Yawkey, they will say yes, because they did. Tom hunted and fished with his friends, and his friends were his employees and the friends of his employees. The employees regularly had meals together they called suppers. Tom paid for the suppers, and his employees could invite guests. If Tom was in town, he would attend the suppers.[60] Of the winter residents, Tom Yawkey was the most approachable, the most social and the most generous.

Ralph and Leila Ford attended Georgetown Presbyterian Church, and in 1955, Leila complained to Tom Yawkey about the condition of the piano in the church. Their son, Ralph, had become the assistant organist in 1944 when he was fifteen years old, and he became the primary organist in 1953. Leila was fully invested in the condition of the music program at the church. After listening to her lament and probably anticipating more complaints, Tom told her to buy a piano for the church and send him the bill. The next day, she and Ralph Jr. went to Seigling Music House in Charleston and bought a reconditioned Steinway grand piano for $1,700. Yawkey paid the bill.[61]

Tom Yawkey also took care of his employees. He wrote two letters to James McLeod, the director of the McLeod Infirmary in Florence, South Carolina, before the hospital was built in Georgetown. One letter was dated 1934 and the other 1944. His stationery address on both letters was 420 Lexington Avenue, New York. Tom lived in the Graybar building, a thirty-story building built in 1927. The Graybar is a limestone and brick art deco building with architectural oddities like cast metal rats on the building support wires.

The first letter was addressed to "My Dear Dr. McLeod" and dealt with an issue that was bothering Tom about his superintendent, Jim Gibson. He said Jim had need of surgery to fix his appendix and that Tom had been after him to go to Florence to have the surgery. Tom said Jim was "like the man who had a leak in his roof. When it rained, he couldn't fix it and when it wasn't raining, he did not need to fix it." He made plans to send Jim to see Dr. McLeod in Florence. He concluded the letter by stating how much he liked Jim, that he was a good superintendent and a "darn good fellow."

The second letter, dated ten years later, was addressed "Dear James." Yawkey first apologized for not attending a quail hunt hosted by James McLeod and then asked about a medical bill that had been pending for Jim Gibson. Tom reminded Dr. McLeod that he paid all of Jim Gibson's medical expenses and those of Gibson's family.[62]

A retired employee of Tom Yawkey tells the story of the same Jim Gibson, who went by the post office one Christmas season to pick up the mail. He tossed a package in the back seat of his truck and forgot about it until after Christmas, when he came across it still in his back seat. The package contained Tom Yawkey's Christmas gift to his wife, Jean. Tom forgave Jim for his mistake, but Jean did not, and she insisted Tom fire Jim. Tom fired Jim but then built a house on Pawleys Island for Jim's large family and gave it to him.[63]

It was obvious to everyone in Georgetown that a house of prostitution existed three miles south of Front Street on the highway to Charleston. Boston sportswriters insist on believing that Tom Yawkey owned the Sunset

Lodge and mention that possibility from time to time, usually in connection to the inaccurate claim that the Boston Red Sox team visited the Sunset Lodge on their way to or from spring training.[64] There have been Internet articles with inflammatory headlines such as "Tom Yawkey's Whorehouse."[65]

There is no question Hazel Weisse owned the Sunset Lodge. The deed for the property and the house was in her name. Tom Yawkey did not own the brothel, but he did lend Hazel $2,700 to buy the house in 1936. Tom told an employee that he never had been paid back for a loan as rapidly as Hazel paid him back, that she would walk into his office with bags of cash.[66] Hazel went on to add to her property in 1937, 1939 and 1941 until she had accumulated twenty acres of buffer around her house. It is likely she made enough money in her business to pay for the additional purchases without borrowing.

Tom Yawkey was thirty years old when he bought the Boston Red Sox, and he was seventy-three when he died. His players were about his age when he bought the team, and it is conceivable he socialized with them and drank with them and invited some of his favorites to his South Carolina property to hunt and fish. As Tom got older, his players did not, and it is likely his invitations were restricted to his older friends, retired ballplayers and associates from the Northeast. As one retired employee said, "Tom Yawkey came to South Carolina to get away from those people [the ball team]; he sure was not going to invite them to come with him."[67]

THE STORIES
AND THE NARRATIVES

INTERNATIONAL PAPER EMPLOYEE

International Paper arrived in Georgetown not a minute too soon. In the middle of the Depression, the company hired 800 workers to build the plant and 1,200 permanent employees to run it. Another 1,000 workers would be in the woods cutting trees. The weekly payroll was $35,000.

One woman graduated from high school in 1941 and then applied for a job at International Paper and was fortunate to be one of the few women hired. She made $110 per month as a clerk, and she said she had no idea what to do with that much money. The first thing she did was to go to Loyal Motors in Georgetown and buy a red 1941 Ford convertible with a white skin top.

"Some of the older men at International Paper resented me. After all, there I was, a young woman—a girl, really—who got a good job and who had nothing better to spend my money on than a sports car. My coworkers were men who had been struggling through the Depression to keep their families fed."

The Depression hit Georgetown County hard; commerce stopped and people struggled. There were men in Georgetown in the 1930s who built roads for the Works Progress Administration (WPA) making sixty-five cents per day. The men who built the Pawleys Island Road had to camp in a tent on a bed of straw from Monday through Friday nights. They built fires for warmth.

Life got a lot better fast when International Paper arrived. Imagine going from making $0.65 per day and living in a tent to making $0.44 per hour for plant workers. If you were a supervisor, you would make $1.44 per hour.[68]

AAAA-1 CREDIT CARD

ISSUED TO

MANY YEARS OF FRIENDLY AND
PLEASANT RELATIONS

Sunset Lodge
GEORGETOWN, S.C.

Sunset Lodge
credit card.
Private collection.

Suddenly, Georgetown got crowded. The population increased from five thousand to eight thousand people, and every spare bedroom in every house and apartment was rented. The newspaper even published an editorial criticizing the residents for their greedy behavior in hiking up rents. Some residents heard the Sunset Lodge went to Georgetown in 1936 because International Paper was about to build the plant, and it is true the steelworkers from Pittsburgh arrived in Georgetown to build the paper mill just a few months after the Sunset Lodge opened for business. Many people in town thought there was a connection between the Sunset Lodge opening for business and steelworkers coming to town.

Everyone at International Paper—at all of its plants around the country—knew about the Sunset Lodge. There was no place like it. Sure, there were brothels in every town, but the madam, Hazel Weisse, ran the Sunset Lodge like the big business it was. She gave away a lot of money to local charities—even more than International Paper. Her clientele was more professional than most brothels. She was a good businesswoman.

International Paper's chauffeur always was available to take a visiting executive to the Sunset Lodge when he arrived from another plant or from New York. The executives tended to stay in Georgetown longer than at other plants. The reason they gave for the longer stays was that the sunsets were so pretty.

The Georgetown paper mill manager even had cards printed that he claimed were Sunset Lodge credit cards. He enjoyed handing out those cards whenever he traveled to other International Paper locations. "Come see us," he would say. "Here, have a credit card to the Sunset Lodge!"

BANK MANAGER

The responsibility of the branch manager in Georgetown was to manage the staff, make loans, open accounts and be involved in town affairs. One banker had a good career with the bank, and as he said, his move to Georgetown to manage the branch was a nice way to slide into retirement.

He knew the Sunset Lodge was in Georgetown, but he never thought about the madam having a bank account, let alone the prostitutes. Going to the bank seems such a natural thing to do, but a brothel seems so unnatural that he was not prepared for his experience in Georgetown.

For one thing, those folks made a lot of money. The madam was Hazel Weisse, and she had a savings account and there always was plenty of money in her account, but the bankers knew her real money was in the trust department in their Charleston office. Her deposits sometimes rivaled or exceeded International Paper's deposits! The money was unreal.

The banker's predecessor set up an arrangement with Hazel to allow her working girls—or, as Hazel insisted they be called, sporting ladies—to open savings accounts. Hazel did not let them set up checking accounts, but they could set up savings accounts and they could buy bonds. Also, Hazel had an address—Route 2, Box 300—that was her official address for the Sunset Lodge, and when a new sporting lady walked in to open a savings account, the teller was supposed to ask no further questions if a woman gave that PO box as her address.

Working at the bank was a real adjustment for the banker. He had been in Georgetown only a short time when a teller walked over to let him know the young woman at her desk worked at the Sunset Lodge. He could not believe it. He stared as long as he felt he could before forcing his head down to look at some papers on his desk. The most remarkable thing about her and the other women who later followed her was how unremarkable they were. They were not flashy or tacky or dramatic. They wore nice clothes but not inappropriate. They could be anyone's daughter. It made him think of the girl's parents and what in the world they would say if they saw her in Georgetown at the Sunset Lodge. As he said, "Candidly, it made me sad."

The tellers always commented on how the ladies smelled. They smelled good—perfume good. He never got close enough to take a sniff, but the tellers could tell him the name of the perfume and how much it cost.

Monday was doctor day and bank day for the sporting ladies of the Sunset Lodge. Everyone knew it. They had to go to town to see the doctor every Monday morning, and they generally spent the morning in town at the bank, at the jewelry store or at the ladies' dress shop. If the banker had to run an errand during the morning, he might see them in the pharmacy or even the bookstore. He always could tell when they were in a store because the store owner practically closed the store to give them his full attention. Some of them went so far as to lock the front door or to post an employee at the front door to keep other customers out. They spent that much money.

Monday also was a big day for deposits at the bank. The women of the Sunset Lodge deposited their cash from the weekend into their savings accounts. It makes sense that Hazel would encourage her women to get the cash out of the Sunset Lodge every Monday; there was a massive amount of money in that building after a weekend. The ladies sometimes bought savings bonds or money orders, and sometimes they just let their savings accounts accumulate.

The women never stayed long in Georgetown, maybe six months to a year. A woman leaving town would stop by the bank, often driving a new car, to close her savings account and get her money, sometimes $8,000 to $10,000. This was in the early 1960s when the average annual income in South Carolina was $3,800.

Hazel often walked into the bank, and she always created a stir when she did. She wore her clothes beautifully, and she always looked good. She was not an attractive woman—she had an unfortunately stern face—but she dressed well, really well, and the tellers who worked there checked out her clothes and shoes and talked about her for hours afterward. Hazels always was generous with her money. She often took presents to the bank for the staff during the year. At Christmas, she gave each employee a gift that cost as much as the gifts they exchanged with their families.

The banker retired and moved away to the house he grew up in. Whenever he told someone where he had worked before retiring, the response always was to ask about the Sunset Lodge in Georgetown. Even now, every story about Georgetown triggers stories about the Sunset Lodge. Still!

FLOWER SHOP OWNERS

A couple in Georgetown owned a flower and gift shop on Front Street. Their daughter grew up in that store, first cleaning the store and then working in the back. Later, when she was in high school, she worked the front.

The daughter loved that the Sunset Lodge was in Georgetown. It did not bother her that other women chose to make their living that way. As far as she was concerned, they could do what they wanted. There was a bit of tension in town among local women who felt a certain marital pressure— that if they did not feel like it then their husbands would head to the Sunset Lodge. As she got older and married, she certainly felt it.

The Sunset Lodge was a famous business, and Hazel brought a lot of money to Georgetown and the business owners loved her. The flower shop owner liked to tell people that Hazel was in a non-polluting, green industry. She was a tourist destination! When Hazel closed the Sunset Lodge, all the business owners and many others were sorry to see her go; oh sure, she would say, the foot-washing Baptists were glad it closed, but not the rest of them.

She knew Hazel well. Hazel was tall and buxom with red hair. She wore glasses. Pretty? No, she had a harsh face, but she was very nice. She was a clothes horse. She had beautiful clothes, and she wore them well. She also spoke beautifully. Hazel went into an insurance office one day, and the receptionist listened to her speak and looked at her clothes and thought she was the wife of one of the northern plantation owners.

Their business was primarily flowers, but they also sold china, crystal and linen. Hazel's girls often shopped there. They bought a lot, and they paid in cash. The owners were like every other business owner on Front Street; they bought inventory for the store with the girls in mind. Having them there was good for business.

The shop delivered flowers to the Sunset Lodge every week. Who from? Satisfied customers! Men sent flowers all the time. It never made any sense to the owner why a guy would send flowers to someone whose friendship he negotiated, but they sold a lot of flowers and they made a lot of money on the Sunset Lodge.

When one of Hazel's girls was in the hospital, they would deliver flowers to the front desk for delivery to her room. They had learned from experience to seal the little envelope that held the card; otherwise, the nurses would peek to see who sent the flowers.

One Easter week, an old man rode up to the shop in a chauffeured car. He walked into the store and bought lilies to be delivered to the Sunset Lodge. The owner was so curious about this man and his interest in the Sunset Lodge that she decided to deliver the flowers to the brothel herself. Now, this lady would jump on a bourbon and water, so when Hazel invited her in for a drink, she was happy to accept. Imagine her disappointment when Hazel gave her a Coke to drink. She had her heart set on that bourbon and water.

She was sitting at the dining room table visiting with Hazel and some of the girls when a buzzer sounded. There was a customer at the back door. The girls headed to the living room to be ready, and Hazel went to let him in. Well, I best be going, the lady decided.

Hazel was a generous person who stayed in touch with everyone in town. When the owners' daughter got married, Hazel saw the notice in the paper, and she stopped by the store for a visit. She told the owner how pleased she was about her daughter's marriage and pulled out twenty-five dollars from her purse and handed it to her and asked her to give it to her daughter as a wedding gift. This was when a twenty-five-dollar wedding gift was a seriously big deal.[69]

Hazel had a birthday party for herself every October. The party was for men only and by invitation only, and men came from all over South Carolina to attend. The party lasted all day, and she gave away everything that day, from drinks to girls. The owner's husband was invited each year; though he never went, they delivered a lot of flowers.

The Sunset Lodge closed in December 1969. Hazel and the sheriff had discussed shutting down the brothel, but he caught her by surprise that

Friday afternoon, and she did not have enough cash to settle up with the girls. She called the owner's husband at the flower shop and told him the sheriff was putting padlocks on the doors and she needed to borrow some cash through the weekend. Hazel's chauffeur drove into their backyard, and the man walked onto the back porch. He shook the chauffeur's hand and handed him the cash. Hazel was waiting in her car on Monday morning in front of the flower shop with the money to pay him back.

DRY CLEANERS OWNER

The dry cleaners owner was about Hazel's age, and they got along well; besides, Hazel did a lot of business with the dry cleaners. The owner was a new widow, and that is why she made time for Hazel and they became friends.

Early on when Hazel first arrived in Georgetown, she seemed determined to set a high bar for an admittedly low-brow industry. She hired the biggest, toughest man in town to keep order at the Sunset Lodge. Hazel turned away the men who showed up dirty after a full day's work at a local construction site or who worked on the ships. Eventually, word got around that this was a brothel with standards. She kept her bouncer until he retired, and she never had to replace him.

The 1940s were more formal than today. Men in business wore suits with vests and hats every day, even the men working at the grocery store. Women wore gloves and hats on Front Street. Hazel required her ladies to wear long dresses and heels every night. They sat in the living room and visited with the men who just wanted to talk. They danced with the men who just wanted to put money in the jukebox and dance. Hazel created an atmosphere at the Sunset Lodge that was very much about the fantasy of meeting and flirting with the pretty girl.

Every morning, Hazel's driver would take armloads of dresses to the cleaners for her to clean and repair. She did not get the sheets and towels; those were cleaned by an industrial company out of Charleston. They would repair any missing buttons, pulled zippers or missing sequins before cleaning the dresses for later pickup. Every one of the Sunset Lodge's girls had several outfits for work.

When one of Hazel's girls was not at the Sunset Lodge, dressed to entertain, she was indistinguishable from any other young woman in Georgetown. If Hazel let her come to town, she would be dressed conservatively with flat shoes, all neat and clean. The stereotypical image of the dramatically dressed prostitute with tacky big hair did not apply in Georgetown. Hazel had to approve the appearance of anyone going to town, and more than once she sent a girl back upstairs to change. Hazel knew the townspeople tolerated her because she did not embarrass them, and she knew better than to rub their faces in her business activities. She never allowed her girls to solicit; if a man wanted to see one of them, he had to go to the Sunset Lodge.

The owner of the dry cleaners usually saw Hazel every week. She would drive to Front Street and park in the same parking space right beside the dry-cleaning store. Sometimes she walked to the bank or the bookstore or the pharmacy, but she always ended up at the laundry to speak to the owner. If she was happy and all was well, she would wave and exchange pleasantries and off she would go. If she was feeling down or lonely, she would stop by the owner's office for a visit. But when she walked in and shut the door, Hazel was low. The owner knew it was time to listen. It was nothing more complicated than that.

Hazel had a challenge living in Georgetown. She was alone in a hostile place; she always had to be on guard. She chose her career and had no one to blame but herself for her problems, but still, she did not have many people she could trust. Hazel always lived on the edge between acceptance and rejection, safety and danger, freedom and jail, relaxation and tension. She made alliances with men who could help her if bad things happened and with men who could hurt her if they wanted.

Hazel was thirty-six years old when she opened the Sunset Lodge and sixty-nine years old when it closed. That is a long time.

Hazel gave away money to ingratiate herself to the community. Giving money was her business model, but it also was her style. She gave to help the hospital, she gave to pay for food baskets at Thanksgiving, she gave to the families of men killed or injured in work accidents and she was an easy ask for anyone raising money for local charities. She liked to give away money and she felt good helping people, but the truth was she gave away money for survival.

OPTOMETRIST

There was an office of optometry on Front Street in Georgetown. Most of the optometrist's customers worked at the paper mill. When they went to see him, they just needed a pair of glasses. Nothing fancy; they just needed to see better. He was happy to set up payment plans for his customers, particularly when they were children who could not see the blackboard. He admitted it was hard to make any money. They called him doctor, but he knew he was just a struggling business owner. He had to buy expensive equipment and an inventory of frames, and he had two employees, one to answer the phone and welcome patients and one to help him in the back. He thought about doing everything himself in the back and just keeping the receptionist, but he did not have the nerve to fire his assistant. This was, after all, a small town.

It did not matter to him one way or the other that Hazel Weisse was out there with her brothel; he did not have any money anyway. From his perspective, at least she didn't put her girls on the street corners or use a hotel in town for her business. She was discreet, so he decided it was okay.

Hazel and many of her girls were his customers over the years, and the difference between them and the paper mill customers was night and day. He knew he could be criticized for saying so, but Hazel was responsible for bringing a lot of cash to Front Street. His spirits lifted when he saw Hazel walk into his shop, and when one of her girls walked in with her, he knew it would be a good day.

Tura advertisement.

Hazel was nearsighted. She was tall, about five feet, nine inches and not skinny and not fat. She was fairly attractive but not head-turning—not someone you would notice on the sidewalk. One thing he noticed about Hazel, she wore nice clothes and accessories.

Every business owner on Front Street stocked inventory with the girls of the Sunset Lodge in mind. There was a limited market for some of the high-end products in Georgetown, but those women made it worthwhile to make the effort to have nice things for sale. Hazel's business was important to the optometrist, and everyone up and down Front Street felt the same.

Hazel was the reason he carried Tura glasses. Tura Eyewear promoted the idea of using glasses as a fashion accessory, and Hazel bought into the concept. Tura was known for jeweled eyewear such as a gold leaf attached to each outside corner of the glasses or, his favorite, a silver accent with blue and clear rhinestones with a unique tear-drop rhinestone that dangled. It was expensive eyewear, but as fashion goes, Tura was the top of the line.

Hazel owned at least a half dozen Tura-designed frames to complement her wardrobe. His optician lived in Tampa, Florida, and he kept asking why one person would have so many different style frames for prescription glasses. The optometrist did not want to get into Hazel's line of work, so he just said she was a woman of wealth who had an elevated sense of fashion.

One of Hazel's girls walked into the shop one day to pick up her order and could not remember the fake name she gave when she ordered her glasses. It was easy to find her order; no one else had ordered two pairs of Tura glasses.

Hazel had a huge impact on the economy in Georgetown County. Business owners on Front Street knew it, and she knew it.

DRESS SHOP OWNER

A widower bought a dress shop on Front Street after his wife died. The Sunset Lodge was good for everyone's business on Front Street, particularly his. You would have a hard time finding anyone in the business district who disapproved of the famous brothel just down the road. The ladies did business with the business owners, and some of the business owners did business with the ladies. The volume of business that the women from the Sunset Lodge did in his store allowed him to employ more people, rent more space and stock far more and better inventory.

International Paper employed a lot of men in Georgetown, but their wives did not shop in his dress store. His was considered a high-end store, too expensive for the lady who needed a dress for church. Some of the wives of the International Paper executives were good customers, though. There was not a female executive class in Georgetown; his business came from the wives of plantation owners, wives of local professionals, women who had inherited money from their families and the ladies of the Sunset Lodge.

The Sunset Lodge had a lot of turnover; it seemed like the personnel changed two or three times each year. That turnover was good for his business; still, he could not imagine where they came from or where they went. Who coordinated all of this coming and going?

A few sporting ladies walked in the shop practically every week. Sometimes they arrived by cab and sometimes Hazel's black Oldsmobile rolled up with her driver behind the wheel. When they walked in his store, the owner dropped whatever he was doing to help them. His oldest saleslady assisted him, but everyone else had to go on break.

How did they know the women were Sunset Lodge ladies? When they walked in, they had a confident air. They knew they could afford to buy whatever was for sale. When they shopped, they did not look at the price tag. They always paid in cash.

Sometimes a girl would buy a dress or scarf or shoes and ask him to mail it to an out-of-state address. All the store owners on Front Street knew what that meant; it was time to pull out the plain boxes and plain wrapping paper. The girls did not want their families to know where they were and what they were doing, but they often bought presents to send home. He would take the store tags off the dresses and neatly pack them in a plain box with no return address. The girl would give the name and address of the recipient, and he would take the box to the post office to mail. That is the way they did business in Georgetown. They adapted.

One year, a teenage boy worked in the store. His dad and the owner were hunting buddies, and the owner could use help keeping the store clean and the storeroom organized. The owner kept the boy out of the way of the customers because women did not want a young man nearby when they were shopping.

One day, the store was quiet, and the two of them idly watched a young woman through the store window. She was standing on the sidewalk waiting for a car to pick her up.

"Fifteen dollars," the owner said.

The boy looked confused and asked, "The dress or the shoes?"

"The girl," he said. "I saw her last night at the Sunset Lodge."

ICE COMPANY OWNER

There was an icehouse in town. Business was very good from the late 1930s until the end of World War II, but as more people bought freezers for their homes, business suffered.

The owner missed an opportunity. Customers already thought of him when they needed to keep food cold, and had he sold freezers and refrigerators along with ice, then he could have been on the ground floor of an important new industry. Understandably, he saw the new machines as a threat to his ice business. He kept on doing what he always had done, and it cost him.

As the potential ice market shrank, he started selling drinks and snacks and even hot dogs to get people into the building. He catered to men going fishing by selling bait along with the ice. Customers even complained about the cost of the ice; they said ice is just water. It became tough making a living in the ice business.

The owner's son went to work for his dad when he turned fifteen years old, and he could tell his dad needed all of the business friends he could find, but he also knew his dad did not approve of brothels. The man refused, as a matter of principle, to do business with Hazel, the madam of the Sunset Lodge. She was allowed to run her immoral business right down the road from Georgetown, and that offended him.

He made it clear to his sons that the Sunset Lodge was off limits. The son did not remember any ice deliveries to the Sunset Lodge, and whenever the topic came up, his dad was quick to be critical. The son respected his dad for his position; to him, prostitution simply was wrong.

One day, a man stopped and asked the son directions to the Sunset Lodge. The boy started to give him directions when his dad called out across the yard asking what they could do for the man and started over. The son told the man his dad would help him, and he walked off. He wanted no part of a joint conversation with his dad about the Sunset Lodge.

BOOKSTORE OWNER

All Cats Go to Heaven. Author's collection.

There was a bookstore on Front Street in the early 1960s. The owner mostly sold hardback books and was beginning to do more trade in paperback. Her bestselling books were novels, followed by biographies and books about historical events. In addition to books, she offered gifts for sale, mostly pens and journals. She carried newspapers and did a good business in Bibles. The churches used her to order Bibles for new communicants and to order copies of books to distribute to Sunday school classes.

The owner did not approve of the brothel in town, but she had to admit Hazel was a good customer. It was strange having her come by every week or two to see what new novels had arrived that she might like to buy. She read a lot, and she gave books as presents. The owner liked to see Hazel come into the store.

Hazel was in the store one morning shopping for a book to read when she came across a book about cats: *All Cats Go to Heaven.*[70] Hazel chuckled at the title. She took the book to the counter to buy, and the owner took her cash and gave her the book in a bag. She thought later she should have asked Hazel if she had any cats at the Sunset Lodge, but she did not think to.

While she was checking out Hazel, another lady walked in and started shopping. When the owner handed Hazel her bag and said, "Thank you, Miss Hazel, come back," the lady's head jerked up to see Hazel, but she already was out the door. The lady ran to the front door to look up the street, but Hazel was walking briskly away, and all the lady could see was Hazel's back. She came back in the store and sheepishly said she had never seen Hazel and was curious to see what she looked like.

SHOE STORE OWNER

The shoe store on Front Street opened in the 1950s. The owner stocked shoes for everyone in town, from the boys and girls in school to the men working in the woods to the moms teaching school to the women buying shoes that looked like the pictures in magazines. He always was on the lookout for shoes that he thought the ladies of the Sunset Lodge would like.

Hazel Weisse was a customer, but she did not often go to the store. Hazel lived in Florence before moving to Georgetown, and the owner believed she bought her shoes in Florence. She had a long, narrow foot. He could have found shoes for her to wear, but it is hard to break a relationship with a previous shoe salesman. She would buy laces and polish and she asked him to repair her shoes on occasion, but he did not get the big sales from her. He liked Hazel and enjoyed visiting with the girls who came to his store. Flirting with them was as close as he was interested in getting to the activities of the Sunset Lodge.

Hazel was very nice but not pretty. She treated everyone the way she wanted to be treated. He had heard she had a temper, but he never saw it. He heard she had a heated conversation with a preacher on Front Street, but that is all he know.

The dry cleaners was next door to the shoe shop. Many times, he watched Hazel's chauffeur carry armloads of clothes into the cleaners to be repaired and cleaned. Hazel often went to the cleaners to see the owner, who he had decided was Hazel's confidant.

When Hazel closed the brothel, it did not mean much financially to the shoe store. His business was pretty strong without the Sunset Lodge business, and other than some shoes he no longer needed to carry, he did not notice any difference. His income stayed about the same when Hazel was there and when she was not there.

FURNITURE STORE OWNER

Hazel knew the owner of a furniture store when she lived in Florence in the 1930s. Hazel moved to Georgetown in 1936, and the owner moved his store to Front Street in 1951. His son worked for his dad as a teenager. Hazel bought all her furniture and mattresses from the store. She was a good customer.

The son delivered mattresses to the Sunset Lodge from time to time. Hazel bought only the best mattresses, Sealy Posturepedic, and she replaced them often. Everything Hazel bought was the top of the line, only the best quality.

The owner also was a customer of Hazel's, and when his son reached a certain age, he, too, went to the Sunset Lodge as a customer. His first time there, the girl took him upstairs and washed him, and he was not ready for that. When he got home, he told his dad he did not tell him everything he needed to know, and his dad just smiled.

They delivered the first color television in Georgetown County to the Sunset Lodge. Hazel put the TV in the living room for the men to watch while they waited to go upstairs with a girl or to watch before going home. Men did not always go to the Sunset Lodge for a girl. There was a large group of men who would go by the brothel to have a few drinks, dance to the music from the jukebox and visit with one another. It almost was like a social club. Sometimes men would eat a meal there. Hazel encouraged men to use the Sunset Lodge as a place to hang around and to play cards.

There were four bedrooms upstairs at the Sunset Lodge. One bedroom was known as the mirror room. The room was not wrapped in mirrors but had gold-framed mirrors over most of the wall space. Those mirrors were made by Bassett and were of excellent quality.

When asked to describe Hazel, the owner said she was tall and thin. She wore glasses. He thought she was a terrific person and a great asset for Georgetown. She ran a clean, professional business. The owner and his son knew Hazel was good to her word. She could order furniture or mattresses over the phone, and they would have no hesitation calling in the order and making payment. She paid her bills promptly and in cash.

The furniture store owner was uncertain if Hazel's brothel was open on Sunday. Neither he nor his son ever went on Sunday, and they doubted if anyone else did either. They said Hazel did not go to their church but they did not know if she went to church. They hoped she did. She was a good person, but she may not have been churched.

The son learned a lot from his association with the Sunset Lodge. His daddy taught him never to put himself in a compromising situation with a woman. He did not want his son to have a woman in his truck who wanted a ride while he delivered furniture to her house. He said nothing good came from casual close association. He said, "Son, it is cheaper at Hazel's."

ANDREWS, SOUTH CAROLINA BANK

Andrews is twenty miles from Georgetown and is one of a few incorporated towns in Georgetown County. There used to be two towns, Rosemary and Harpers Crossroads, that were combined, incorporated and named Andrews in honor of an employee of the Atlantic Coast Lumber Company.

Andrews suffered like Georgetown during the Depression. The town had two main sources of income: the railroad and the lumber company. The railroad cut back its schedule at the beginning of the Depression, and then the lumber company closed in 1932. The economy in Andrews was as bad as or worse than it was in the town of Georgetown. It was tough for the residents.

There was one bank left in Georgetown County after 1929, and that bank was in Andrews. The family who owned the bank struggled to keep it open. A town that loses its bank loses everything. It was hard on the family to lend money it did not have, and the business owners and farmers in town desperately needed help.

It sounds odd, but fortunately for them, Hazel Weisse opened a house of prostitution in 1936 in Georgetown County. She was a money machine, and she brought much-needed cash to the county. She could have kept her cash in her house or used a bank in Charleston, but she trusted the bank in Andrews. The suspicion was she knew her deposits into the bank would make the difference in its survival, and she was correct. Once the banks opened again in Georgetown a few years later, she moved her banking relationship back to Georgetown, but the people of Andrews appreciated that she was there when they needed her. They have nothing bad to say about Hazel Weisse.

Hazel would get into her car every Tuesday and drive to Andrews to make a deposit. From the Sunset Lodge, she had a twenty-mile drive on a poor-quality road. She would arrive in Andrews and park in front of the bank, and the tellers would have been watching for her. Only men were tellers in those days, and their normal business attire was a suit with a vest and a hat. A teller would walk out to her car, and she would hand a bag of cash through the window. He would count the cash inside and make a deposit and hand her the deposit slip, and she would drive off. She never got out of the car. The family who owned the bank considered her relationship with the bank to be the beginning of drive-through banking in South Carolina.

PLANTATION OWNER

I own a plantation in South Carolina." At home in New York, that was a pretty nice brag. The northerners of means knew the history of South Carolina plantations and the story of Bernard Baruch with his sixteen thousand acres and Tom Yawkey with his twenty thousand acres and Archer Huntington with Brookgreen Gardens and George Vanderbilt with Arcadia Plantation. Most plantations were nowhere near as big, but that was okay; the small plantation owner had servants who worked for almost nothing, and he had a place to take friends to hunt.

There were about three dozen northerners in the Georgetown area who owned plantations. None of them was from South Carolina. A few local men, realtors and attorneys who benefited from the sale and purchase of local plantations, started the Carolina Plantation Society to give them advice and a sense of belonging but mostly to encourage their friends in the Northeast to buy more plantations.

The Depression was not that tough on most of those men who were wealthy, and some of them took advantage of the pain to buy a plantation or to buy more plantations to increase their holdings; however, the Depression created challenges for plantation workers in South Carolina.

The banks had closed in Georgetown County, and it was not in the plantation owners' best interests to have a frantic and scared local population. Each man handled his plantation differently. Most of them hired more servants than they needed, and they built a bunch of stuff they otherwise would not have built. They bought as much product as they could think of from local businesses. It was unbelievable the brick walls in Georgetown County that they paid for. They even set up a free infirmary for the Negroes.

The best place in Georgetown for the northern plantation owners was a store on Front Street that catered specifically to their needs. It started out as a grocery and hardware store and later expanded into a marine and hardware store on one side and a grocery store on the other. Those guys would do anything. They fancied themselves as a S.S. Pierce–type store, the famous store that opened in 1831 in Boston. Schooners came into Georgetown with lots of goodies for the rich. The benefit of the store to the plantation owners was the variety of services the owner offered. They were able to get cash charged to their accounts, and they could request special items to be ordered. Archer Huntington bought a donkey from them and later bought a car and had both charged to his account.

The plantation owners used the river system in Georgetown County as their roadways. When they went into town on their boats from the plantations, they would stop by the store and put in their grocery and hardware orders. The men at the stores would fill the orders, load the orders onto the boats and charge the entire thing to their accounts while they shopped on Front Street.

On Saturdays, they sent one of their bigger boats with their employees to Georgetown to get paid. They set up the store as their paymaster, and the store owner added the payroll to their accounts. Upon arrival, the employees would go into the store; white people went in the front door, and the Negroes went in the back door by the water. Everyone got "paid," but what tended to happen was they would use the store credit to buy sugar and flour and maybe a hoe. They seldom left with any cash money.

There are many examples of the creativity of the Front Street businesses during the Depression. When Archer Huntington built Brookgreen Gardens, he needed somewhere on the rail line to unload statues for the gardens and for large supplies. The hardware store owner opened a building materials store on Fraser Street where the railroad was, and he became the responsible party in Georgetown for receiving goods by train and delivering them to Brookgreen.

One plantation owner said, yes, he had heard of the Sunset Lodge, and he heard some plantation owners called the madam to ask for women to entertain at parties they hosted for visiting hunters. But he said, "I never did."

MARINA MANAGER

T here was a marina on Front Street in Georgetown. Front Street runs alongside the Sampit River. Four rivers dump into Winyah Bay, and a fifth joins the Atlantic Ocean below Georgetown. The Intracoastal Waterway enters Winyah Bay by way of the Waccamaw River, and the marina was in the ideal place to take advantage of river travel.

The marina manager appreciated that Hazel Weisse was in Georgetown; she was great for business. A ship captain had a choice of places to stay on the Intracoastal Waterway, but the marina manager could compete with any marina on the East Coast. Everyone on the water knew about the Sunset Lodge, and men would plan their business and pleasure trips to stop in Georgetown.

The marina manager's favorite realization of the economic benefit of the Sunset Lodge to the marina involved the ship captains for the owners of yachts that would "break down" in Georgetown. The owner would tell his captain to take his boat from New York to Miami, and the boat could not complete the trip without a few days of repair in Georgetown. The manager had to go to a captain on occasion and ask him exactly what he wanted the manager to put on the bill to send to the yacht owner as the reason for the repair.

The marina was a busy place, at least in Georgetown. Everyone from rich kids to television and movie celebrities to mafia men docked at the marina, needing gas and a hot meal. The manager handled hundreds of dockings every year, and he seldom saw the owner of a yacht, usually just the captain. There were pleasure boats from Miami to Boston stopping at the marina. He would charge them to tie up for the night, and they would buy gas and get a shower.

The marina was on Front Street within walking distance of everything a man would need; however, a guy needing a brothel had to ride three miles to visit the Sunset Lodge. There was a store on Front Street that sold groceries, ship stores, building materials and marine hardware. There were doctors and clothing stores and department stores and optometrists and even a flower shop. There were restaurants and banks. The Plaza Theatre and the Strand Theatre were an easy walk up Front Street.

One day, two young fellows arrived in an expensive forty-seven-foot sport fishing boat. The marina manager was impressed. The slightly older one was the captain, and the college-age-looking fellow was the mate. They spent the late afternoon cleaning the boat and then cleaned themselves up to get ready to go out. The manager gave them the name of a restaurant down the street, and he heard the captain tell the mate about the Sunset Lodge experience they would enjoy after dinner. They must have had a good time because the next morning two beautiful girls from the Sunset Lodge hopped on the boat with them. The captain told the marina manager they were going to the marina at Fernandina Beach, Florida, about a day away, and they would drop off the girls to get a ride back. There is no doubt those girls had no trouble getting back up the coast, if they even came back.

It seemed like every day a yacht or pleasure boat would tie up and the captain would ask how to get to the Sunset Lodge. In the 1960s, the chauffeur for the Sunset Lodge would take guys there from the marina and bring them back, but in the 1950s, the manager often drove them and waited in the dining room of the brothel and then took them back. He did not mind; the tips were huge. Nowadays, you are fortunate to get a $5 or $10 tip, but then, he routinely would be tipped $50 or $100, and one night he was given a $1,000 tip. This was in the 1950s!

One man who worked in Georgetown often took customers to the Sunset Lodge and was rewarded with a spend-the-night party. He was a fishing guide who built in a trip to the Sunset Lodge in the schedule for his customers. Hazel knew he was taking customers back and forth, and they got to know each other as they sat at the dining room table waiting for his fellows to finish their business. One night, she walked over to the man and told him to take his guys to his boat and then come back, that she would like to give him a girl for the night as a present. He could not wait to drop the guys off and hightail it back to the Sunset. It has been fifty years since that night, and he can still tell stories as if it was last night.

GROCERY STORE OWNER

There was a grocery store on Front Street from the late 1890s until it closed in 1966. Three generations of men owned the store. The man who opened the store lived until 1936, his son lived until 1958 and the grandson closed the store in 1966. Each man had an impact on the town.

In the early days, the owner stocked his store with goods brought in by schooners. Some people in town did not shop there because they said the products were too expensive. The store owner built a dock on the river with steps into his store so the plantation owners could tie up at his dock. By the time the first owner died in 1936, he knew all the rich northern men who had moved to Georgetown County to hunt ducks on the old rice plantations.

The plantation owners came to Georgetown to hunt and fish and to entertain their friends. They learned to rely on the store to run their plantations. There was one well-known story about an employee who made a mistake and forgot which of the plantation owners had ordered a saddle. The store owner told his clerk to bill all the plantation owners, and the one who bought it would pay the bill and the rest would let him know he had made a mistake. The punch line of the story was that they all paid the bill.

The grocery store was important to Georgetown. By the early 1930s, the store expanded by opening a marine and hardware store. with connecting doors to the existing grocery store. Two sons of the owner split the management responsibility; one son ran the hardware store, and the other son ran the grocery store.

The grocery store was the only job the grandson ever had. When he was young, he helped the men put the grocery orders in the boxes and loaded them in the cars. Before telephones and cars, women would stop by the store to drop off their orders, or they would send a servant. A clerk then would deliver the groceries to their homes in a horse-drawn wagon, and if no one was home, he would go in and put the perishables in the icebox. As more homes bought refrigerators and more homes had telephones and as the owner bought cars for the store, it became easier to do business. By the 1930s, they were taking orders over the phone, filling them and delivering the boxes to the homes in station wagons.

There was a lot of big news in the mid-1930s in Georgetown County. International Paper built the paper mill, the new bridge opened over the Pee Dee and Waccamaw Rivers and Hazel Weisse arrived in town.

Hazel Weisse started slow. She bought that big Dutch Colonial house down Highway 17, and somehow, she hired women to work for her. Anyone could have run her off when she was new in business, but the store owners always heard Tom Yawkey had something to do with her being in Georgetown. Within a few years, Hazel was making as much money as virtually any woman in South Carolina, and she knew how to reinvest her money in the community. It was not long before everyone in town had been impacted by her presence.

Hazel did business with as many business owners as she could in Georgetown. She did her banking in Andrews while the Georgetown banks were out of business during the Depression, but otherwise, she was Georgetown loyal. She did right by the owners of the grocery and marine stores. She knew and did business with the son of the owner and the grandson, covering the years from 1936 when she arrived until the store closed in 1966.

As the grandson got older, he and Hazel developed a close friendship. She would go into the store every week or two and they would talk; they shared a lot of interests. Hazel loved fashion, and she had multiple pairs of eyeglasses, beautiful glasses by Tura Eyewear. Not many men had heard about Tura, but he knew all about the company. He thought Hazel's clothes were just lovely. He loved to talk about the latest fashions with her.

The grandson's mom taught him to play the piano when he was little, and later he learned the organ. He played the organ at the church in Georgetown for over fifty years. One day, he offered to play an organ at the Sunset Lodge during the evenings. No, Hazel said, we do not need any more organs being played at the Sunset Lodge.

Commerce in Georgetown, like a lot of towns, suffered in the late 1950s. The grandson was twenty-nine years old when his daddy died in 1958. The store had spiraled down when his daddy was sick, and the grandson was not seasoned enough to take over. When the man died, the store was in debt, and the grandson had to learn quickly how to be a businessman. He turned it around, and by the time he sold the store in 1966 to a company in Charleston, they again were in the black. He was proud of that.

Hazel Weisse was a loyal customer, and her business meant a lot to the store's survivability. She served a lot of food every day at the Sunset Lodge. She generally had about six sporting ladies there plus her chauffeur plus several black ladies who did the cooking and cleaning. There were about a dozen people eating three meals every day. Generally, the chauffeur took the shopping list every morning to the grocery store, and he would get the mail and run errands or even go to Charleston before coming back to pick up the food. If necessary, one of the men at the store would take the order to the Sunset.

One day, her chauffeur walked in the store with the grocery list written on the back of a cleaner's receipt. The grandson flipped it over and read what items Hazel had paid to be cleaned: a dozen towels, a dozen hand towels, four dozen washcloths…

People in Georgetown knew Hazel was generous, and they saw her name in the paper from time to time giving money to Easter Seals or the March of Dimes. She did a lot more anonymously; of course, people talk, and there are no secrets, so word got out. She gave the grocery store money every fall to make thirty Thanksgiving baskets to deliver to the poor families in Georgetown. She also gave money to take care of families who had a death or injury. Whenever they asked him who gave the money to buy them food, the store owner would not say, but people knew.

WESTERN UNION

In Georgetown, there was a Western Union, the telegram company that specializes in money transfers, money orders and business payments. During the 1940s and 1950s, there was a steady flow of business from folks in Georgetown who wanted to transfer money or send telegrams. A Western Union telegram was so much faster than the post office mail that a telegram came to mean important and urgent. Sadly, many families received telegrams during World War II to let them know of the deaths of their soldier sons and daughters.

There were a lot of telegrams and money orders from the Sunset Lodge. There were sporting ladies from the Sunset Lodge who showed up every week to take care of personal business. They had to use their real names, of course. Sometimes a girl would send a telegram, and sometimes she would wire money. Usually, a cab would take a couple of them to town and then take them back. They were courteous and friendly, and they always were nicely dressed. The madam, Hazel Weisse, told the manager that if anyone from the Sunset Lodge received a telegram, he should call a cab and send the telegram. The cab ride was paid by the girl receiving the telegram.

One time, the Georgetown police chief and a U.S. marshal from Charleston walked into the Western Union office while the manager was there. The marshal was investigating one of the girls, and he wanted to know her full name, how much money she was wiring and the name of the person to whom she was wiring the money. The manager had been well trained, and she told them she would not share that information with them and that if they wanted her to cooperate then they had to have a warrant. They never came back.

Hazel herself walked in occasionally to send a telegram or wire money. Of course, the manager knew her; everyone knew Hazel.

HEATING AND AIR OWNER

There was a small heating and air business in Georgetown. The owner installed units and responded to service calls. After a few years in business, he added a helper to carry stuff, particularly those big fans up shaky steps to the attic. After a few more years, he had enough money to hire a technician who could take his place while he went to new customers to give estimates. He then picked up another helper, so he had two teams when times were busy. Most days, he stayed in the office or went out to generate new business while his teams were responding to calls.

There was one time the owner always went by himself, and that is when Hazel called from the Sunset Lodge. In his experience, every business in town gave Hazel the owner's attention. She was too important and too wealthy and just too interesting for the owner not to go himself. He considered she had a brothel, for crying out loud, right there in Georgetown County that everyone knew about and no one did anything about. A brothel with prostitutes. Oh, she did not call them that, he knew; she called them "sporting ladies." But who was kidding whom? She had the county around her little finger, and no one said much about it. He observed that she gave money to charities, she spent a lot of money with local businesses and, who knows, she may have even "bartered" her services for the services of the business owner. The heating and air company owner would not do that; he did not have much money and none for that sort of foolishness.

Anyway, he went out there one day to install an air conditioner in one of the windows at the Sunset Lodge. Hazel always bought the top-of-the-line product, and she always paid him in cash. It was a hot day in the summer, and she was more than glad to see him show up. She did not like her customers to be uncomfortable. The window unit he needed to replace was downstairs in the living room where it looked like men waited to go upstairs to the bedrooms. There was a jukebox and two really long sofas. There were a few girls in the living room talking; if he had not known where he was, he would have thought they were just young women visiting friends. He was there on a Thursday afternoon. It was not nighttime; it was the afternoon, and he was surprised to see some guys coming into the living room. It was odd. Here he was working while these guys—well, they were playing.

He noticed one sporting lady who went upstairs with one guy, and he got to work on the window. He had to take the old unit out and put the new unit in the window and put an aluminum sheet around the rest of the window and then caulk the unit so cold air could not get out and hot air could not get in. He did not have his helper that day, as the job did not require any heavy lifting and he did not want to see him standing around watching the action. So it took him a bit longer to finish the job. By the time he left, that same girl had been upstairs three times. The owner calculated Hazel's fee and the girl's net income and compared it to his fee; she made more money while he was at the Sunset Lodge than he did!

GIRL SCOUT

Many people grew up in Georgetown and knew nothing about the Sunset Lodge. Girls sometimes heard a little something, usually from the boys who may or may not have known much about it. Later, in high school, the girls would hear the boys bragging about going to the whorehouse on Saturday night, but the girls never believed it. One night, a group of girls was riding around town and decided to go to see the Sunset Lodge for themselves. They were scared driving over the bridge in Georgetown and heading south.

On that night, they pulled into the driveway at the wagon wheel by the road and drove around the back of the house honking their horns and laughing; it was fun but unnerving. They giggled and talked all the way back to Georgetown about their experience. It seemed silly later, but at that time of their lives, they were stepping out!

There were some boys, the bad boys, who the girls thought probably did go to the Sunset Lodge. They were the edgy guys, the guys who the girls would not go out with but who they would dream about. Girls heard the madam would take a young boy's money like any crusty old ship captain's money; if a male had fifteen dollars, he was a preferred customer.

Anyway, growing up in Georgetown was special. The town was safe, the teachers were nice and the children loved and were loved. The boys played baseball, and the girls would gather at their games to visit with one another and to see and be seen. Many girls also joined the Girl Scouts and had a good time.

Everyone knew about the cookie sale each year; that was the primary fundraiser for the Girl Scouts. The Girl Scouts had been selling cookies for forty years, so the process was simple and repetitive; the girls went to their neighbors and asked them to buy cookies for the benefit of the Girl Scouts. They took orders for cookies and picked up the cookies when they arrived at the house of the mom who was in charge that year, and then the girls delivered them to their customers.

Simple as it was, one girl was a bit young her first year to know what to do. Her mom refused to do it for her, so she put off the cookie solicitations until the day before the deadline. Her mother told her to go to their neighbors on the town side of their house, that a girl who lived a block away already had canvassed their neighbors on the other side. That is what happens in a small town; the moms split up the territory among themselves, and the neighbors simply wait for one of the girls to ask for the order.

This girl was a bit overwhelmed. She did not want to knock on doors and ask her friends' moms to buy cookies; it was embarrassing. Also, one of the bad boys in her class lived between her and town, and there was no way she was going to knock on his door and run the risk of him answering the door!

Her brother got his driver's license that summer, and he cared about little more than driving around town. He heard their mom lecturing his sister on responsibility and commitment, and he told her he knew a place where she could sell cookies and be done with it at one house. It was three miles away on the road to Charleston, and he would be glad to drive her there if she gave him a box of cookies for his room. She did not know all cookie boxes were accounted for, so she said sure, he could have a box. And they went.

They pulled over in front of the house, and she walked by herself past the low brick wall and the overgrown camellias and the cedar tree to the front door. She had no idea she was knocking on the door of a brothel and that the customers used the back door. She later discovered the only people who knocked on the front door were lost.

A tall, stern-looking woman answered the door, and when she realized the young girl was selling cookies, she invited her into the living room. The room had two very long sofas and a jukebox. The girl had never seen a jukebox in a living room before. Later, she would enjoy playing songs at the Whistling Pig, but as a Girl Scout, she was too young even to know what a jukebox was. The lady ordered a *lot* of cookies, and then ladies showed up from upstairs and gathered around her looking at the list of cookies and ordering boxes and boxes. People have asked the girl what the ladies were like, and all she can remember is how pretty they were and nice. They smelled good too.

That was the Girl Scout's experience with the Sunset Lodge. She has a good memory of her visit. She won an award that year for the most cookies sold, and the Sunset Lodge was the only place she went. She realized later that a woman in the brothel business can work up an appetite for cookies.

FATHER AND SON

This is the story of a father and son. It takes place in the 1950s when the relationship between fathers and sons tended to be more distant, less touchy and a lot less communicative. The boy played sports, and his dad would attend some of his son's games. They hunted and fished together when the dad and his friends were not going away for the weekend. The father's life did not revolve around his son. If they did not have sports and hunting and fishing, the son was not sure what they would have talked about.

At home, the boy's mother took care of his sisters and the house and his dad took care of him, which suited the boy fine. They liked to do the same things, and he always was happy going anywhere his dad was going. In those days, schools did not get a lot of holidays, but for some reason he had a holiday on a weekday, so his dad told him the night before to get his gun and fishing gear ready.

They were in the tree stand an hour before daybreak, the boy's favorite time of day. He had learned early, even at age twelve, not to make any sudden movements while hunting. His dad could sit in a tree stand motionless for hours. He would take thirty minutes to turn his head to look from the left side to the right. The boy moved around a bit but not much. On this morning, the boy was a sixteen-year-old, seasoned, camouflage-wearing hunter who enjoyed being outside waiting for a deer.

On that day, at that time, in that place, the deer were safe. The hunters waited until the sun was up and the temperature was making them a bit uncomfortable in their hunting clothes and then headed to a general store that served breakfast. For a sixteen-year-old boy, this was about as good as it gets. They ate a big breakfast, drank coffee and visited with the men who were coming in from hunts. Everyone had a story to tell. Some were successful and some were not, but everyone had a satisfied look; this is where they wanted to be.

After breakfast, the father and son peeled off some of their outerwear and went to a nearby pond to fish. The fish were biting that morning, and they had a nice string of bass and bream to give the caretaker on their way off the property past his house. They stopped back by the general store to clean up and get a sandwich for lunch and then drove toward home.

The boy remembers like yesterday the moment he realized they were not going home. His dad turned instead of going straight, and his son asked him where they were going; all the man said was, "It's time." The boy had no idea where his dad was taking him, and when he figured it out, he was scared to death.

Nothing else was said on the drive to the Sunset Lodge. The boy sat in the passenger seat and could not think of a thing to say. He was petrified. The man slowed down, turned into a driveway and drove around the back of a large house. He knocked on the back door, and a tall lady opened it. Just to the left of the door as they entered was a small bar. Dad's friend Rupert was sitting at the bar drinking from a paper Dixie cup. Dad ordered a bourbon, and the boy was underage, so he got a Coke.

The boy thought about that Coke over the years. Here he was in an illegal place of business about to break several laws with his dad, and Hazel was not offering him alcohol. That is one reason, he believed, Hazel Weisse lasted so long; she stayed focused and did not take unnecessary risks. From his perspective, it was a good thing he did not have a bourbon. He was scared enough without adding alcohol to his system. His dad paid one dollar for a Coke when the general store probably sold it for a dime.

Rupert and the boy's dad sat in the bar drinking out of Dixie cups while he sat off to the side, sipping his Coke and getting increasingly nervous. After a while, his dad told the madam, Hazel, that this was his son's first time and asked if she had anyone who could take care of him. A girl appeared. The boy did not know if Hazel pushed a buzzer or left the room or if she asked someone to go get her. He was almost unconscious with fear.

The girl told him her name, and they went upstairs. She was well dressed— not a gown and heels but neat, classic. It was early afternoon. She took him into a room with a bed and sink. On the floor was a stack of white enamel pans. She partially filled a pan with warm water and told him she would have to wash him first with soap and water. He never got to the bed. He was about to hyperventilate. If she had touched him again, he would have fainted. She tried to help him overcome his embarrassment, but nothing was working. She finally said, "Let's go downstairs."

His dad and Rupert were still at the bar, drinking whiskey, when he and the girl returned. Dad asked his son if he wanted another Coke, but the boy had seen his dad's reaction to the first one-dollar Coke; besides, he desperately wanted to leave. His dad drank the rest of his bourbon and stood up, spoke to Rupert and turned to go out the back door. Before he opened the door, the girl touched his arm, leaned up and whispered in his ear, "He tore out my guts."

FIRST TIME

There are many coming-of-age rituals. By far the most personal of these rituals is the first time for a young person. A boy grew up in South Carolina, and when he turned fourteen years old, he was able to get a daytime driver's license. He started exploring his world, driving by himself to see and to do. He had heard about the Sunset Lodge, but he was unclear how it worked, what it cost and exactly what happened there. He asked a few older boys where it was and what to do, and after being teased a bit, he discovered this place, this unbelievable place, was within his range to drive. He could get there and back, leaving after school and returning home before his family expected him.

When he told the story many years later, he candidly said he was scared to death. He drove around the back one afternoon, parked his car and rang the bell at the back door. He did not know if he would be held until his parents arrived, if the police would arrest him or even if his mom would be standing by the car when he walked back out.

A tall lady answered the door, and he met Hazel. She invited him in, took one look at him and said, "You have not done this before, have you?"

"No, ma'am."

"What is your name?"

He told her.

"Do you know Jimmy?"

"Yes, ma'am, he is my daddy."

"Do you know Dan?"

"Yes, ma'am, he is my uncle."

"You tell the truth," she said and told him to wait there. She came back and said she had picked out the right girl for him. She said she wanted this to be a special event in his life.

He does not remember much about the girl, but she took him upstairs and explained that she would have to wash him and why. Of course, that was all it took, but she kept him in the room and they stayed quite a while. It was a great experience. He does not know what Hazel told the girl, but Hazel did not want him to be embarrassed or humiliated.

He then became a regular customer of the Sunset Lodge. His preference was to drive to Georgetown after school. He would go by the Sunset Lodge, pick out a girl and get his business done. He was of the opinion that most guys did not hang around; they showed up for one thing and left. The price was ten dollars. He went one afternoon with ten dollars in his pocket and the price had increased to fifteen dollars. He told Hazel he did not know the price had gone up and he only had brought ten dollars; he would have to come back later. Hazel pulled him in and said, "That's okay, you are a regular. For you, today, ten dollars."

He did not worry too much about getting any diseases, but it was important to him that the girls had certifications of good health under the glass beside the bed. He understood they went to the doctor every week and were certified.

As he remembers it, the women did not stay at the Sunset Lodge long at all. There was a lot of turnover, but he does not know where they came from or where they went. There were about six girls there at a time.

A few years later, he moved to Myrtle Beach and worked at the Myrtle Beach Pavilion, and he remembers Hazel coming to the Pavilion with children. He assumed they were her grandchildren or nieces and nephews. She pulled him aside and told him not to offer her a free pass. As she said, when he went to see her, he paid full price and when she went to see him at the Pavilion, she paid full price.

He still considers that Hazel was an asset to Georgetown County. She ran a good, clean business, and everyone respected her. He never heard a negative thing said about her. There was no trouble at the Sunset Lodge—no shootings or stabbings or big fights. Hazel would not put up with misbehavior.

BLEMISH

One man was a business owner on Front Street, and he freely admitted that he profited by Hazel being in Georgetown County and was sorry to see her close. He said you can talk about the immorality of what was going on at the Sunset Lodge all you want, but the truth is the town benefited economically from her presence. She spent a lot of money in Georgetown businesses, and she gave away more money to charities than any person or business in the county.

Hazel's business was a tourist attraction, a destination. She kept her business activities three miles from town at the Sunset Lodge, and she did not embarrass the town. She did not let her sporting ladies solicit on Front Street, and he heard she would not allow them to look a man in the eyes when in a store or on the sidewalk.

He realizes why Hazel Weisse set up her business in 1936 in Georgetown when he thinks of the economic impact of International Paper arriving in town in that year, the new Georgetown bridge completing the Coastal Road from Maine to Florida in 1935 and the final cut completing the Intracoastal Waterway from Virginia to Florida in the late 1930s. She might have had to leave Florence or just wanted to, but whatever happened in Florence, she picked the right place to move when she chose Georgetown.

He identified the problem with Hazel and said there was no way to excuse it: Hazel served minors. This man talked to men who were as young as fourteen years old when they first showed up at Hazel's door with money in their hands. Hazel would let them in. He said it was and is inexcusable. Those boys were old enough to have a driver's license but were not emotionally mature enough to be able to handle an adult situation.

This man financially loved that Hazel was here and believes she did a lot for Georgetown, but he thinks her treatment of minors is a blemish on her time in Georgetown, and he is ashamed it happened.

DEPUTY SHERIFF

Georgetown County has a sheriff's office, and the City of Georgetown has a police department. They generally work well together, but they have different responsibilities. A deputy sheriff worked for three sheriffs during his career in Georgetown County. One sheriff allowed the Sunset Lodge to open in the county, one sheriff allowed it to stay open and one closed it down.

This man was a young pup in 1935. The people in the county were suffering during the Depression, and he was grateful to have a job. There was huge excitement when International Paper announced the construction of the paper mill in 1936. You would have thought they had just won a war, and in some ways, they had.

He remembered sitting in the sheriff's office for their Monday morning meeting after the announcement. He was giddy that jobs were coming to Georgetown. Also, the bridge across the Waccamaw River and Pee Dee River was finished, so at long last they could drive north to Virginia on the Coastal Road without getting on a ferry. Ferries are nice when the weather is nice and the water is calm.

The sheriff told them big changes were coming to the county, and he was right. The first thing that happened was the steelworkers from Pittsburgh showed up to build the paper mill. Construction of the mill started in October 1936, just a few days after the project was announced. Suddenly, the police and the sheriffs were busy. Those guys were not like local men. They rode around the county looking for something to do, and candidly, they were a rough bunch. The deputy sheriff was wearing a badge, but it still suited him fine for them to build the paper mill and then go back where they came from. International Paper was motivated to complete the mill quickly and had access to as many workers as it needed; surprisingly, the mill was open in nine months, and sure enough, the steelworkers went home.

There is a story line that the county leaders let Hazel Weisse come to town with her brothel to distract the steelworkers, and it is true that the dates work out. Hazel bought a house that was three miles south of Front Street in September 1936 and was open for business when the steelworkers arrived in October. It was obvious the sheriff had no plans to chase her away. The deputy did not understand it. There would have been nothing to shutting her down. He could have ridden down there, arrested everyone in the house and padlocked the door, and that would have been the end of it.

Another thing he did not understand was what Tom Yawkey had to do with it. In 1936, Yawkey was one of the fifty richest men in America. The deputy kept hearing that Yawkey owned the Sunset Lodge, but how much sense did that make? He certainly did not need the money. The sheriff told him that story was not true, that Yawkey lent Hazel the money to buy the house and land, and that made sense. Maybe that is why no one bothered Hazel's business—she was under Yawkey's protection. Better him than organized crime. All the deputy knew was that life in Georgetown got better for everybody when International Paper arrived, and no one seemed interested in discussing the illegal house of prostitution in the county.

The deputy's second sheriff had zero interest in closing the Sunset Lodge, and if anything, he helped Hazel by shutting down other brothels that tried to open. More than once the deputy was sent to a building in the county to shut down a house of prostitution and arrest the madam, but he was never sent to the Sunset Lodge. Friends asked him if Hazel paid the sheriff to let her stay open, and he said he did not know anything about that. The deputy knew for a fact he never got anything and he never saw anything.

One funny incident happened when the sheriff's new preacher went to him and said the Sunset Lodge was a sinful place and had to be shut down. The sheriff looked at him and said, "Sunset Lodge? Where is that?"

The third sheriff was appointed by the legislative delegation. He ran for his own term and was elected, and then in 1968, he ran unopposed for reelection. During his 1968 race, he promised he would shut down the Sunset Lodge. What protected it for so long? As far as the deputy sheriff was concerned, the sooner it closed the better. It appears the sheriff looked at the situation in Georgetown and in American society and decided enough was enough. Georgetown in 1968 was not the same place as when Hazel arrived in 1936.

The sheriff knew Hazel's health was not good, and he could see the end. Hazel had turned over management of the Sunset Lodge to Pat, a longtime employee, and based on comments the sheriff made, it was understood that Hazel was not happy with Pat's standards.

The sheriff and Hazel were friends. It was easy to see her confiding in him, particularly when she got sick. Also, she read the newspapers when he ran for sheriff in 1968. She knew his plans. He had talked to her about her situation going forward. He knew her plans.

In the fall of 1969, on a Friday afternoon, the sheriff told his deputy to go with him, that he wanted a witness. They drove south on Highway 17 and pulled around the back of the Sunset Lodge. Hazel answered the door, saw the sheriff standing there and said, "Sheriff, come in, I have been expecting you."

The three of them sat at the dining room table, and the sheriff said, "Hazel, it is time."

Hazel nodded and she indicated she knew and agreed. Some people asked the deputy if this meeting was for his benefit, that maybe Hazel and the sheriff had already worked out the plan. He did not think so, but like he said, Hazel and the sheriff were friends.

Hazel thought the sheriff would shut her down that day. She started to ask him for a couple of days to pay the girls and to let them leave on their own, and he held up his hand and said, "Hazel, you do not have to close now. Let's agree on two months. Within two months, you will close."

She nodded, and that was it. No big threats, no screaming, just two friends cutting a deal. Hazel did not have a warm, hugging female personality, so there were no hugs between them—just a nod and a meeting of the eyes.

HOSPITAL NURSE

Before there was a hospital in Georgetown, there were nurses. Medical care in Georgetown was difficult in the 1940s without a hospital. There was a small hospital for the black residents, but it only had a few beds. Even smaller Kingstree had the Kelly Hospital, but it took Georgetown until 1950 to build its first hospital. If someone in Georgetown needed more medical attention than one of the six doctors in town could provide, he or she normally rode seventy miles to McLeod Hospital in Florence or sixty miles to Roper Hospital in Charleston. In an emergency, an ambulance with a driver and a nurse would take the patient either south to Charleston or north to Florence.

One nurse who predated the hospital worked her entire career in Georgetown. She knew Hazel Weisse. She thought Hazel did a lot of good in town, and the town folks appreciated her. There was no tension in Georgetown with her out there. The nurse thought so highly of Hazel that she recently told a city councilman that he and the city council needed to get that place going again.

The girls from the Sunset Lodge were patients in the Georgetown Hospital from time to time, and Hazel would visit them. Peggy, one of Hazel's girls, was beautiful but very ill. Peggy was afraid she would die or, if she did not die, that her parents in Virginia Beach would find out she was a sporting lady at the Sunset Lodge. Peggy recovered, and Hazel sent the nurse a beautifully wrapped present at the hospital from a very nice women's clothing store. The other nurses made her open the present at the hospital; inside was a long white silk dressing gown with lace and accordion pleating. From that time on, the clothing store owner would tease her about her Sunset Lodge connection.

Hazel commanded respect in Georgetown. She was generous; whenever there was a crisis, Hazel was there. The nurse remembered a mill fire that killed three men. Hazel provided food and money to their families and then presents at Christmas. Hazel gave money to everybody, it seems, including the churches, but no one ever remembers seeing her in church or hearing of her going to church.

After the nurse retired, she moved to Charleston and lived at Ashley House. After Hazel closed the Sunset Lodge, she continued to live in her garage apartment behind the closed brothel with a black lady who took care of her. The family who bought the Sunset Lodge building as their home watched out for Hazel, but eventually Hazel moved to Charleston and was a neighbor of the nurse at Ashley House. Hazel was on the eighth floor and the nurse was on the third.

One day, the nurse stood waiting for the elevator. When the door opened, there was a stretcher and two attendants, so she stepped back to let the door close, but they said there was room, so she got on. She did not look at the person on the stretcher, to respect the person's privacy, but she heard her name and it was Hazel.

She worked part time at the St. Francis Hospital in 1974. She was Hazel's nurse when she was a patient before she went to Indiana, where she died.

IRS AGENT

T he men and women who work for the IRS are assigned territories to live and work. The IRS agent who lived in the Georgetown area for a while was the regional officer. He would receive a list of businesses and individuals each week to audit. The Sunset Lodge was in the county and, therefore, his responsibility. He said he never had a problem with Hazel Weisse.

Hazel filed every form on time and paid every tax and fee. The sporting ladies were 1099 employees and listed their occupation as hostess on their tax returns. The IRS does not care what someone does for a living as long as the IRS gets its share. They have no interest in calling the police to report an illegal business. They just want the business to pay up.

He heard a rumor that Hazel was stung pretty good in the early 1950s by the IRS. They have formulas to determine income, even for brothels, so if someone is suspected of understating business income, the IRS can estimate the actual taxable income. The story is the local IRS agent in Georgetown at the time got the Sunset Lodge's receipts from the laundry and calculated a taxable income for Hazel that was far higher than she admitted. He counted the number of towels, sheets and washcloths at the laundry and figured the income to assign to the Sunset Lodge, and he handed Hazel an enormous tax bill.

The challenge any business owner has in a dispute with the IRS is fighting a presumption of income. The burden of proof shifts to the taxpayer. Hazel's problem was compounded by the nature of her business. It is unlikely she kept records of specific customers, but she must have kept records of the number of customers each sporting lady entertained each day so she could accurately pay them. If she kept those contemporaneous records in a file, and if the result was consistent with her tax return, there would be no problem. Apparently, there was a problem.

The rumor is she went to see her friend Tom Yawkey and explained her tax problem to him, and he paid or helped her pay the tax, but it is impossible to know if that story is true. Another rumor is that she went to a South Carolina politician who she knew and asked him to approach the IRS for her and help make the tax bill go away. Again, those are just stories.

The Georgetown IRS agent went to the Sunset Lodge one day to see one of the hostesses about her taxes. He knocked on the back door, and Hazel answered, wearing a house coat and leaning on the door frame. She said, "What can I do for you, Honey?"

He never will forget it.

"What can I do for you, Honey?"

The confidence, the posture, the voice.

One day, the IRS agent received a call from the wife of an IRS co-worker who lived in the Northeast. She was looking for her husband, and she called the operator and asked for the number of the Sunset Lodge. The operator said there was no number. She told the IRS agent she did not understand it; her husband said he always stayed at the Sunset Lodge in Georgetown on his way to Florida.

MINISTER

The residents of Georgetown are and always have been a religious people. They have built and supported churches of different Protestant denominations, along with Catholic churches and Jewish synagogues. One man was the minister of a large Georgetown Protestant church while Hazel Weisse owned the Sunset Lodge. He had been at churches before in towns that had episodic problems with brothels, but the police did their jobs and shut them down. He occasionally had to counsel men in his churches who were frequenting the local house of prostitution, but they would work through the issues together. He never had been in a town like Georgetown.

The people in his church simply did not seem to care that there were prostitutes in town. He asked the other ministers, priests and rabbi in Georgetown, and they had the same reaction from their congregations—no one cared, even the women! The few times he challenged a church member about the Sunset Lodge, he or she would just shrug and, to make matters worse, sometimes would make a comment about all the good that madam did. He tried to get a group of church members together to meet every month for a Bible study to pray for the purity of the town and to pray for forgiveness, but he could not keep it going.

He became convicted of the need to get rid of the Sunset Lodge. It was unbelievable what went on in that building. Men would walk inside and pay money and pick a girl to take upstairs! Some of these men would be from other towns, and some were from Georgetown. All of them were lying to their wives, and many of them were with girls the age of their daughters. It was horrible.

He organized a group of like-minded ministers in Georgetown, and they went to see the sheriff. They insisted he shut down the Sunset Lodge. They told him the brothel was the primary source of family strife in Georgetown and that it was his responsibility to close an illegal business in the county. They told him the Sunset Lodge was a den of sin that was a cancer on our society.

The sheriff listened until they all had a chance to express their outrage that such a place would be tolerated in Georgetown County. Then he said, "Ministers come and go, but we have to live here. Send me your elders and your deacons and I will shut it down."

Well, there was no way they could get their church officers to go see the sheriff, so the minister kept on preaching and kept on working against the Sunset Lodge. He walked out of a store on Front Street one day and there was Hazel Weisse, the madam of the Sunset Lodge, walking out of the store next door. She took one look at him and told him to leave her and her business alone. She said she was an excellent corporate citizen of Georgetown and that she did not appreciate his efforts to close her down. It was shocking. He did not know what to think.

DEPUTY POLICE CHIEF

The Sunset Lodge was in Georgetown County, not the city of Georgetown, and that suited the deputy police chief fine. He did not want to answer questions from visitors about why a brothel was allowed to exist in his town.

The city police station was on the ground floor of the clock tower on Front Street, which worked out well. Everyone knew where the clock tower was, so everyone knew where there would be a city policeman. The sheriff's office was on the edge of town, and those guys were responsible for the unincorporated areas of Georgetown County from Murrells Inlet to the town of Andrews. The Sunset Lodge was in the county, three miles south of the town of Georgetown, on the way to Charleston on Highway 17.

There is a great story about a young man who was looking for the Sunset Lodge when he had a fender bender. The county sheriff took him and his friend to the Sunset Lodge while the car was in the shop and then picked them up when the car was ready. That story did not surprise the local police at all. The truth was many of the law enforcement officers, city and county, were customers of the Sunset Lodge. No one thought anything about it; certainly no one thought that Hazel should have been arrested. That just was not the way the people of Georgetown County looked at the situation. Hazel arrived in Georgetown when International Paper was under construction and those Yankee steelworkers from Pittsburgh were roaming up and down Front Street. At least that is what the deputy police chief heard; he worked for the police department in the mid-1960s, which was thirty years after Hazel arrived in Georgetown. She was untouchable by the time he got there.

The marina on Front Street was just a block down the street from the city police station. Boats and ships were arriving every day, and a lot of the ship captains and owners were heading to the Sunset Lodge.

One day, a boat arrived with two couples and their dogs. The wives wanted to walk down Front Street and shop, so they told their husbands to walk the dogs while they were gone. The husbands hooked up the pups to leashes and walked to the police station to see what there was to do in Georgetown. It did not take long for the conversation to turn to women and then to the Sunset Lodge and then to the guys leaving their dogs in the back of the police station while their owners got a ride to the brothel. The women returned to the boat to discover their husbands and dogs gone. After waiting a while, the women got worried and walked over to the police station to see if the officers had seen their husbands. They described the men and the dogs and asked where they could be. The officer took the ladies out to the front of the building so the dogs would not start barking and assured them their husbands probably were fine but to make sure, he would drive around the area to see if he could find them. He drove straight to the Sunset Lodge to get the men and returned them to get the dogs and go back to the boat.

One thing the city and county law enforcement officers can agree on: there never was any trouble out there. Hazel took care of her business and did not allow anyone in her building who had been drinking to excess or who was belligerent. Old-timers tell stories about a bouncer in the early years, but it was clear to all that Hazel Weisse did not need anyone to protect her. She was a powerful woman who knew how to control men. She did not want any trouble because trouble is bad for business and Hazel was all about business.

CAB COMPANY OWNER

The taxicab company was owned by a couple who met in the military and moved to Georgetown, where they bought the only cab company in town. They soon realized the Sunset Lodge, located three miles down Highway 17 toward Charleston, was going to be great for business. They had eight cabs at the peak of Hazel's popularity, but when the Sunset Lodge closed in 1969, they reduced the fleet to four cabs.

Often, men would park their cars in restaurant parking lots and one of the cab drivers would pick them up there to take them to the Sunset Lodge. Sometimes the driver would wait for them and sometimes the customers would let him leave, but that was okay; there always was someone who wanted a ride back to town. The driver could charge five dollars per ride because the Sunset Lodge was outside the town limits. Men who arrived in town on yachts would tie up at the marina on Front Street, and if the marina manager was too busy to take them to the Sunset Lodge, they would call a cab.

Georgetown and the surrounding areas have a long history of men taking taxicabs to the Sunset Lodge. In the 1940s, Charleston cabs would pack in as many soldiers as could fit and drive an hour to the Sunset Lodge. The cab driver would sit in Hazel's driveway and wait until the soldiers were ready to leave, then take them back to the base.

The girls used cabs to get to town; Hazel did not want them to use their own cars. A cab would pick them up—usually two girls, never more than three—and take them to the dress shop, the beauty parlor or their weekly appointment with the doctor. According to the backseat conversations the drivers overheard, Hazel would not let the girls go to town in groups, and she was particular about how they looked. On occasion, one would complain about having to change clothes before Hazel would let her leave the Lodge. The cab drivers got the impression they would vent when they were safe in a cab, but they were not about to buck Hazel's authority. What Hazel said, went.

The cab drivers also ran errands for Hazel. If Hazel did not want to eat the food prepared and left by the cooks at the Sunset Lodge, she would call them to pick up steaks at the Lafayette Restaurant for her and the girls. Even as other cab companies competed in business, Hazel liked these folks because they were professional with the girls. One time, one of the drivers treated one of Hazel's girls with disrespect, and the owners fired him. Hazel appreciated that.

A favorite destination was the jewelry store on Front Street. Hazel would call ahead on behalf of the girls, and the jewelry store owner would be ready for them. One day, the cab driver and two girls arrived at the store and the owner got in the front seat with two or three trays of his best jewelry. He showed them what he had picked out for them, and they chose their favorites. No money changed hands.

Their other driving responsibility was to drive Miss Hazel's black Oldsmobile. Hazel would call for a driver to drive her car to town. It was rare for anyone to get out of the car but Hazel. She generally had two girls with her. Based on the conversation in the car that the driver reported to the cab company owners, they learned Hazel would take the newest girl at the Sunset Lodge to town to give her a tour of Front Street and explain the rules.

There were a lot of rules. Hazel cared about everything. She wanted the girls to dress modestly. She told them not to look at men on the sidewalk and not to acknowledge knowing them. She told them never to draw attention to themselves. She told them they could not leave the Sunset Lodge without her permission. She said they could accept an overnight job but never in Georgetown; they had to go at least to Myrtle Beach.

The cab company was one of the few businesses in town that had Hazel's unlisted phone number. Some of the nurses at the hospital had Hazel's number; doctors often played poker at the Sunset Lodge, and in a medical emergency, the nurses had to find their doctors. Some of the appliance repair guys had her number as well.

The couple who owned the cab company heard everything from their cab drivers. They often sat around during quiet times and told Sunset Lodge stories. One of the drivers even saw a couple of girls get on a boat and leave with two men. He was called to the Sunset Lodge one morning to take two girls to the marina, where they hopped on an expensive sport fishing boat. They told him on the way to the marina that two men had been at the Sunset Lodge the night before and had invited them to go with them to Florida. The girls were looking forward to sunning on the deck and enjoying the day on an expensive boat. The wife of the cab company heard that story from her driver, and all she could think was, oh, to be young and beautiful.

NEW SUNSET LODGE OWNER

When Hazel decided to close the Sunset Lodge in 1969, she was in poor health, and she did not want to be on the property by herself. The couple who owned the cab company in Georgetown had a pleasant working relationship with Hazel. They were a young couple with two children, a girl twelve years old and a boy four years old.

Hazel asked the man to stay in the Lodge for a few nights in case customers stopped by. Hazel wanted him to tell them to leave. She then asked the couple to buy the property if she could continue to live in her garage apartment. They had a conversation about the building, and they decided to buy it as their home; however, they could not afford the purchase price. Hazel agreed to finance their purchase. They bought 4.3 acres in 1970 with a four-bedroom house plus a few outbuildings that the working girls had stayed in. The young couple had to pay Hazel $150 per month for sixteen years and ten months. They put down $1,000 and financed $19,000.

It was strange moving into a brothel. The four bedrooms were upstairs, and the cabins were scattered around the property. There was a garage apartment that was Hazel's home. There was a pink log cabin in the back that was used by Marie from Louisiana, the prettiest girl the wife remembers seeing out there.

The young wife was intimidated by the beauty of the women at the Sunset Lodge. She was self-conscious when she moved into the former Sunset Lodge building with Hazel living in the back because she did not think Hazel would consider her pretty.

They bought Hazel's house furnished. She just walked away. There was food in the cabinets. There was a large living room with two one-hundred-inch sofas and four chairs. There was a cigarette machine in the dining room and a beautiful dining room table with chairs. A Coke cooler with a sliding top held the alcoholic drinks in the dining room. There was a jukebox at the bottom of the stairs and a gorgeous buffet with a mirror. Tom Yawkey used to take his dog and visit Hazel on a white leather armless chair at the bottom of the steps.

There were jars of keys on the buffet, and no one knew why. The bedrooms did not lock. Hazel wanted to be able to respond if a girl needed help, and there was an intercom system for the rooms upstairs and the outbuildings. She could listen to make sure everything was okay. Each bedroom was furnished with beautiful pieces, and everything had a glass top. There was a vanity in each bedroom.

At the top of the stairs was a cedar chest that Hazel loved. When the young couple moved in, Hazel told them not to let anything happen to that chest. Men used to sit on that chest while they waited their turn.

The dining room table was the only table. The kitchen was too small to have a table, so everyone ate in the dining room. With a half dozen or more girls working for her, Hazel had a lot of people to feed three times every day. There was a gas stove in the kitchen and a double-door refrigerator. The phone was hidden in the pantry behind curtains.

The cost of "going upstairs" was three dollars back in the 1930s, but the price increased to twenty dollars for thirty minutes when the couple bought the property. Hazel would walk down the hall knocking on doors to let the men know their time was up. There were four bedrooms upstairs and one bathroom, and there were enamel pans stacked in the bathroom, some of which the new owners kept. They did not make many changes to the house, but they did replace the mattresses.

Hazel made it known to the captains of the ships that came into Georgetown that the captain and his ship managers were welcomed but not the men who worked on the ship. She tried to maintain a professional clientele. She would not let a man into her building if he had too much to drink or if he was dirty. She served only white men, and there were no black girls.

Hazel was ready to close the Sunset Lodge in 1969. The story is she went to see the sheriff and offered him the credit for shutting her down. However it happened, the sheriff came in unexpectedly and gave Hazel and the girls until 3:00 p.m. to leave the premises. The girls got out quick; the new owners know this because they used the drawers of the chests of drawers as their suitcases. When the couple moved in, most of the chests were missing their drawers. Over the next year, most of the drawers found their way back to the house as the girls dropped them off or sent them by friends.

The Sunset Lodge closed on December 16, 1969, and the new couple bought the property on January 6, 1970. Hazel gave them permission to move into the house in mid-December before they closed the loan. A Catholic priest started coming around after they moved in to talk to Hazel about giving him the property to start a boys' home. The wife was plenty annoyed that he tried to take the property from them; Hazel told her to keep him from seeing her, so she did.

The wife took care of Hazel while she lived in the garage apartment. She lived back there with her good friend, a black lady, but Hazel had to be moved to a nursing home in Charleston three years later. The couple went to see her one day in Charleston, and it was sad. Hazel said to the husband, "You have your pickup truck. Please put me in the back and take me back to the Sunset."

He said, "I'm sorry, Hazel, I cannot do that."

In 1974, Hazel was taken to a nursing home in Indiana, where she died.

It took a few years for word to get around that the brothel had closed. They had ten cars a day stop by the house looking for the Sunset Lodge. The men who walked or drove into the backyard invariably were embarrassed and polite. One man walked into the backyard as their children were riding down slides on blankets and toys were in the yard. He looked around and said, "I'm not in the right place, am I?"

One day, a busload of soldiers from Fort Jackson in Columbia rolled into the backyard, and the husband walked out to chat with them and let them know they had wasted a trip. The couple worried about the safety of their children. That is when they decided to block the circular drive around the back of the house.

The husband dug in heavy posts on either side of the driveway and hung a heavy chain. One day, a man drove right through the chain and heavily damaged his car. The man ran over to make sure the driver was okay and asked him, "Didn't you see the chain?"

The man said, "Yes, but I did not believe it!"

The husband died in 1991. In 1993, the widow was on a trip when someone broke into the house, stole some guns and started a fire. The headline in the *Georgetown Times* said, "Fire Claims One of County's Most Infamous Landmarks. Old Sunset Lodge, State's 'Best Known' Brothel, Burns." Everything in the house was destroyed.

ARC LIGHT IN A WHOREHOUSE

From Barnwell Blarney or Colonel Frank (Clio Press, 1945), Remembered by Eugene N. "Nick" Zeigler

Hugh Willcox recalled that he and Colonel Frank went down to Pawleys Island in October 1954, after a hurricane named, by odd coincidence, Hazel. They drove down to the coast to talk to an insurance adjuster about compensating Hugh for the damage that had been done to his beach house by the hurricane. On the way back to Florence, Colonel Frank decided that they should stop in Georgetown. He directed Hugh to turn into a strange driveway and park. They were at the Sunset Lodge.

According to Hugh, Colonel Frank never said a word, but got out of the car, went to the back door and knocked. As Hugh put it, "Directly somebody opened the door and it was this nice-looking lady. It was Hazel. When she saw Frank standing on the back steps, she jumped about that far off the floor and grabbed him around the neck.

"Oh, Colonel, I'm glad to see you. I'm glad to see you. You've been away too long!"

Colonel Frank told Hugh to join him and they went into the Lodge's kitchen. Hugh recalled that "Hazel knew the Colonel wanted a drink, so she broke out a jug of liquor and put it in the middle of the kitchen table. Then she summoned all the little girls* from upstairs to come down to the kitchen.

---

* In Rebecca Godwin's novel, *Keeper of the House*, the black maid employed in an establishment like the Sunset Lodge tells the story. She refers to the prostitutes as "the hoes." I remember that any adults I overheard discussing the red-light district in Florence in the 1930s did not use the word "whore." They spoke of prostitutes and bawdy houses in a red-light district. Hugh Willcox's use of the euphemism "little girls" in describing the prostitutes was typical of the time. Perhaps the word "whore" had too earthy and sensual a sound for proper conversation (page 144).

And so we sat around there and fixed a drink apiece, and the little girls all came down and fixed a drink a piece."

And the Colonel started telling a lot of his stories and had them all laughing and giggling and carrying on. And that went on, I guess, for 30 or 40 minutes, and they were having a hilarious time, those little girls were. Then Colonel Frank said, "Colonel Willcox, ole Colonel Barnwell may be a candle in polite society, but he's an arc light in a whorehouse."

BELLMAN

The Ocean Forest Hotel in Myrtle Beach was a magnificent building. It was a ten-story hotel with two five-story wings, completed in 1930. The owner could not make the mortgage payments due to the impact of the Depression, and his New York lending bank foreclosed on the property. The hotel was not cared for properly after World War II. It was getting a bit tired looking by the 1960s, and the age and condition of the building were obvious even to the fraternity members who went there for beach weekends, but it had a wonderful history.

A student from the University of South Carolina worked as a bellman during the summers while he was in college. He claimed to have learned as much at the Ocean Forest as he learned at the university. There were working girls in Myrtle Beach who would arrive at the Ocean Forest, check into a room and go looking for the bellmen to ask for referrals to men who were staying at the hotel that night.

The bellmen did not have to do business with the girls, of course, and some of the guys chose not to get involved, but this student was all about the money. The girls tipped him a couple of bucks for every referral. Occasionally, one of the ladies would offer to barter with him, but he had better things to do with his money. He never understood the appeal.

Life got interesting when the girls were busy and guys were standing there in the driveway asking for a girl for the night. The bellman would tell them about the Sunset Lodge in Georgetown, and they could decide if they wanted him to take them there. It was a thirty-mile trip.

He made the trip to Georgetown more often than not. The difference between the girls at the Ocean Forest Hotel and the girls of the Sunset Lodge was obvious to the guys going back and forth. The girls in Myrtle Beach were locals who were sneaking over to get a room at the hotel and who were subject to arrest if the police ever cared about arresting them, which they never did. The girls at the Sunset Lodge were professionals, not locals, and the customers went to them. Hazel Weisse, the madam, kept a small footprint in Georgetown County. She did not let her girls solicit business, and she trained them to be as invisible as possible when they were on Front Street.

The bellman would drive the guys from the Ocean Forest to the Sunset Lodge, which gave him a good bit of time to visit with them and increase the likelihood of a large tip. He would sit at the dining room table at the Sunset Lodge to wait for his guys, and then he would take them back. He got to know Hazel Weisse. It seemed a long way to go for an evening out, but that is what happened. Men will do anything.

ROBBERY

Men—and the few women—who worked at International Paper put in long hours, and they did okay financially. One man who worked there reported he made enough money to rent a house and raise a family, but there was not much left over at the end of the week. He had been to the Sunset Lodge a couple of times, both times just to have a drink. He did not go upstairs. As he said, "Who has a spare ten dollars?"

The Sunset Lodge was the only place to go in Georgetown to get a liquor drink unless the man joined a private club. There were no bars in town. A guy who wanted to drink had to buy a pint or a half pint and go home to drink it or hang around with his buddies somewhere. Of course, it was illegal for the Sunset Lodge to have a bar, but hey, this was a whorehouse where everything was illegal.

It had been a long week, so the man decided to go by the Sunset Lodge after his shift at IP to get a drink and maybe another. He got paid that day. There were a half dozen guys there, all locals, and the atmosphere was festive.

Hazel let in a fellow through the back door who they all recognized but not well. He announced in a loud voice that this was a robbery and to give him their money. They laughed! What was this guy doing? He pulled out a pistol, and they stopped laughing. They put the contents of their wallets in a bag, and out he went, into the night. The man was stunned. That was his weekly paycheck. What would he say when he got home? What would he do for food for the next week? One of the men in the room wanted to go after him, but Hazel yelled no, to let him go. She said he was armed and for him to do something like this, he must be desperate.

There was talk of calling the sheriff. The men in the room did not know Hazel had a telephone in the pantry, so they talked about driving to a phone to let the sheriff know who robbed them. Hazel said no one would be calling the sheriff; she told them she would make up their losses and she would pay their bar bill and each of them had a free trip "upstairs." That turned them around. They no longer cared about finding the guy who robbed them and eagerly began to anticipate the evening fun.

Everyone said Hazel ran a good business, and she did. Everyone said she controlled her business environment, and she did. The police said they never had any problems at the Sunset Lodge. After the robbery, those men knew why.

FRATERNITY INITIATION

A freshman in college in 1959 pledged a fraternity. Each of the pledges was given a task to complete, sort of a treasure hunt. It would be nice to report an uplifting task such as delivering a meal to a shut-in or fixing an old lady's screen door, but these were boys telling boys what to do. The freshman's job was to go to Georgetown with another pledge brother, get a napkin signed by the madam of the Sunset Lodge and have breakfast with the girls at the brothel.

The boys left Columbia early one morning and drove to Georgetown, turned right onto Highway 17, crossed the bridge, drove three miles and looked for the wagon wheel out by the road. They drove around the back and rang the doorbell. A tall woman about sixty years old opened the back door, and they started to explain why they were there. She held up her hand: "Fraternity initiation?"

They nodded, and she pulled open the door. "Come in."

There were a couple of girls sitting at the table eating breakfast. One boy looked at the buffet against the wall, and there was regular breakfast food in serving dishes: scrambled eggs, sausage and pancakes. He does not know why that surprised him, but he still remembers the food they ate. They sat down and drank coffee and visited. The girls were really pretty, and the freshman's buddy started chatting up one of them. This boy was too shy and frankly a little overwhelmed.

The boy was ready to leave when his friend asked for the keys to the car. He gave him the keys, and off he went. He was gone forty-five minutes while the boy sat there watching some girls finish breakfast and other girls start breakfast. He filled up on coffee and sat there contemplating how odd life is when his buddy came in and asked him if he was ready to go. He was way past ready. They thanked Hazel and walked to the car with their signed napkin safely in the boy's pocket. He looked in the back window to see his spare tire was in the back seat.

"Why is the spare tire in the back seat?"

"I tried to sell it. That girl cost twenty dollars. They only offered me ten dollars for the tire."

DISHWASHER

South Carolina State College in Orangeburg is a historically black college. The young woman who lived next door to Miss Hazel's chauffeur and errand man was looking for a summer job while she was home from school. The chauffeur knew she was looking for work. He offered to hire her to wash dishes at the Sunset Lodge. She did not know she had been hired to work in the kitchen of a brothel, but she needed the money, and it did not bother her to be there.

There were several black ladies who cooked the food at the Sunset Lodge, and she was there to clean up. She and the chauffeur would leave their houses at 7:30 every morning, and he would drive around town picking up the other ladies. They worked from 8:00 a.m. until 4:00 p.m. After work, he took them home, in reverse order. They did not work on Sundays.

They were there to cook and serve food to the employees of the Lodge. There were about a half dozen prostitutes plus Miss Hazel and the fellow who worked in the yard plus the kitchen ladies—about a dozen people every day. They also fed breakfast to the men who paid extra to spend the night with one of the girls.

The big meal of the day was lunchtime, the meal people in the South call dinner. There generally were not many customers at midday, and Miss Hazel and the girls were more relaxed. Sometimes a few girls were on Front Street shopping, but they were not allowed to eat in Georgetown, so they always got back to the Lodge in time to eat.

After cooking dinner and cleaning up, the ladies started cooking food for Miss Hazel and the girls to eat later in the day. Their schedules were determined by the men, and it got busy after men got off work, so they made food that was easy to get out of the refrigerator when the girls had a minute to eat. They cooked enough food for twenty people in case men were playing cards and wanted something to eat or Miss Hazel wanted to invite a regular customer to stay to eat. After they cleaned up, the chauffeur took them home.

The college student enjoyed her work at the Sunset Lodge. Miss Hazel did not allow her to go into the living room, so she did not see much. When she arrived in the mornings, she went through the back door and into the kitchen, and she stayed there until it was time to go home. When Miss Hazel was not there, she would peek through the kitchen doors when the back-door bell rang to see if she knew anyone. There was one man she recognized as a business owner on Front Street. He arrived at the Lodge three times each week, always at lunchtime.

The ladies in the kitchen went to the same church. One would start singing while she cooked, and another would join in and then the others. The girl sang too. Think of it—black women in the kitchen of a cathouse, cooking and singing hymns!

SPORTING LADY

She worked for the Sunset Lodge for two years during World War II while her husband was in Japan. She was a young bride from Alabama. As soon as her husband shipped off, she was stuck in Charleston by herself and lonely for her family. She went to work at the shipyard, but it was dirty, the hours were terrible and the money was not much; besides, she was a good-looking girl who was surrounded every day by guys on the prowl. She fell for their pitches a few times, but she got tired of feeling used and she got tired of being poor.

One day she drove to see Hazel Weisse at the Sunset Lodge. Hazel was working in the yard when she drove up. She introduced herself and told Hazel she wanted to work for her, and Hazel invited her to sit at a small table in the kitchen to talk. They visited for a couple of hours, and the girl ended up telling Hazel about her husband in Japan and the men she worked with at the shipyard, and she cried a bit. Hazel was nice, but she was all business. She asked her a lot of questions, many of them very personal. Hazel told her in detail how it would be every day at the brothel. She told her sometimes she would not feel like it and sometimes she would not like her job. She told her about the customers and said the men would choose her, that she would not have a choice in the matter. Oddly, she never talked about the money, and the girl finally had to ask her. Hazel said if she liked her job or even if she just tolerated her job, the money would be unbelievably big, but if she did not like the job, then no amount of money in the world would be enough to make her do it.

They agreed on the terms of her employment. She would get free room and board, and Hazel would pay her one-half of the five-dollar customer fee. Hazel required she live in the house and be available to customers all day and evening until 11:00 p.m. unless a man wanted to spend the night with her, and then she and Hazel split the twenty-dollar overnight fee. She was required to wear a gown and heels every night. She did not have any nice clothes, so Hazel took her to a dress shop on Front Street, where she picked out five gowns and shoes to match. Hazel paid the bill and said she would deduct the cost of the clothes from her first paycheck. The girl did not even notice the clothes deduction from her pay.

She made a lot of money. Her $2.50 share times her daily activity added up. No one made $7.50 per day in South Carolina in the 1940s, and the truth is she made a lot more than that. Hazel hired a lady to sit at the bottom of the steps to take the men's money before the girls took them upstairs. One night, the lady whispered to the girl that she already had fourteen check marks beside her name that night. Wow!

GEORGETOWN PHARMACY

Girls in high school in Georgetown in the early 1960s had a hard time finding a job that the boys did not automatically qualify to have. One high school student interviewed at the pharmacy and was hired to work after school most days, but she played sports on Saturdays. The owner of the pharmacy was a member of the well-known and influential Lebanese community in Georgetown.

Most customers called in their orders and prescriptions by phone, and a black fellow who worked for the pharmacy made the delivery to their homes on a bicycle. Some customers walked into the pharmacy and placed their orders and waited for one of the employees to fill the order, and others left to shop on Front Street and would stop back by to pick up their packages before going home. The pharmacy had a wide variety of products available that most stores did not offer at the time, such as batteries, skincare products, hair brushes and toothpaste. And perfume.

The girl's primary job was to work behind the drink counter and serve Cokes and other soft drinks from machines that had pre-mixed ingredients, but if the pharmacy got busy, she would help fill orders and wait on customers.

She later admitted to being embarrassed it took her so long to realize who the women were who shopped at the pharmacy and spent so much money. She was not a naïve individual, but it simply did not occur to her that the women who walked into the pharmacy were prostitutes at the Sunset Lodge; it just did not register. Everyone in the store talked to them and about them in such a familiar way that it was a given who they were.

The women were well dressed and wore makeup and perfume—lots of perfume. There never were more than two or three ladies in the store at a time. They bought powder and makeup, and the girl never had seen bottles of perfume as large as the bottles they stocked at the pharmacy. These bottles were not your typical 2.5-ounce bottles; they were huge.

She did not work at the pharmacy in the mornings, so she was not there when the ladies arrived to place their orders. They usually shopped on Front Street for most of the morning and stopped back by the pharmacy to pick up their packages. She did not know specifically what was in the bags, but she never had seen anyone else spend $200 at a pharmacy in the early 1960s. For the average person, $200 would be a two-week salary.

No wonder the owner of the pharmacy catered to the madam and the ladies of the Sunset Lodge. When they walked in the store, the delivery guy on the bike parked across the front door to keep other customers out. The girl was told she had to stay behind the drink counter. The pharmacist himself picked up their bags and carried them to Hazel's car, which usually was parked out front. If they forgot to request a product, he would help them.

The girl never saw money pass hands, and she did not know what to make of that. Maybe they paid for their orders in the morning when they picked out what they wanted. Maybe Hazel paid once every month. She just did not know.

TENNESSEE VISITOR

A young couple in Tennessee dated while they were students at the University of Tennessee. The girl's daddy was the president of the bank, and the boy was just trying to get through school. He liked his potential father-in-law but found him to be a bit intimidating. He was sort of a black-or-white, right-or-wrong sort of man. The boy sought out the man's advice one time about a conflict he was having with his brother, and the man helped him see how he was being unfair and unreasonable. He went to his brother and apologized, and they became a lot closer.

He and his girlfriend were still dating other people occasionally, but they both thought they could be happy being together long term. He wanted to get his first job, and she was thinking about graduate school. He was a senior at the University of Tennessee, and she was a sophomore.

A group of fraternity brothers decided to go to Myrtle Beach for a golfing weekend in the spring of their senior year at UT. They piled into a few cars and headed to the beach. It is hard to imagine now, but that was the time of life when guys would pop open a beer in the morning before getting out of Knoxville.

They played nine holes the afternoon they arrived in Myrtle Beach and started up the grill that night and cooked steaks. The next day, they played twenty-nine holes and had a few drinks afterward. One friend mentioned that the Sunset Lodge was thirty miles south and wondered if the others wanted to go that night. They all knew what it was; everyone knew what it was. He let the group decide; he was not going to be the guy who said no.

They got into their cars about 8:00 p.m. that night and headed down Highway 17 to Georgetown. One of his fraternity brothers had been there the year before, and he told the other three in his car all about what to expect. He told stories, and by the time they passed through Georgetown, there was a lot of tension in the car. The boy was getting nervous.

There were cars parked everywhere, mostly in the woods in the back but there were a few cars near the building. The boy almost passed out when he recognized one of the cars. It had a Tennessee license tag and a dent in the back left corner where his girlfriend had backed into a tree one night in her driveway. His potential future father-in-law was in the Sunset Lodge, and he was about to go in.

It was not going to happen. There was no way he was willing to step into that building and come face to face with his girlfriend's father. He would be terribly embarrassed to be seen by the successful bank president, but more importantly, he could not do that to his girlfriend's dad.

He told the guys in his car to enjoy themselves, that he would stay in the car. He slid down in the seat and stayed put. His friends returned to the car an hour later looking mighty pleased with themselves and chatting up a storm. He looked over to the building, and the car with the Tennessee tag was gone.

NEVER SAY SARDI [71]

New Yorkers Found Lodge with the Sheriff's Help

ARTICLE BY JACK LELAND IN *GEORGETOWN TIMES*, APRIL 17, 1985

One Spring day in the Big Apple, the boss decided that one simply couldn't visit New York without at least one meal at Sardi's, the Broadway beanery so well known to the famous of stage and screen. It was a Monday evening, and there being no theatre that night, the huge main room, with its caricatures of the greats of today and yesteryear—including film star Ronald Reagan looking down—was not crowded at all. A rather nice-looking man, in a well-cut suit with a brocade vest, showed us to our table. Later, hearing him greeted by patrons at nearby tables, I realized he was "The" Vincent Sardi, son of the founder of the famous restaurant.

After dinner, while awaiting my wife in the lobby, he approached me and observed: "I see you are wearing your North Main Woods red suspenders." I had not realized they were so easily visible under my grey flannel coat.

"Oh Yes." I answered, "I've been buying them from LL Bean for many years."

With that, he unbuttoned his vest and, lo and behold, he had on the same sort of galluses.

Of such incidents are introductions made and pretty soon he knew I was in town on a lecture trip, that I was a newspaper man and that I hailed from the Palmetto State.

"Ever know of a place called Georgetown," Mr. Sardi asked and, when I admitted to having grown up in McClellanville, he waxed eloquent.

When he graduated from high school in the 1930s, his father let him have a convertible automobile for a trip south. With a classmate, he was headed for Florida and registered at the former Ocean Forest Hotel, then the Grand Strand's only hostelry. The two youths had come down Highway 17, the "Ocean Highway," the main travel route between New England and Florida at that time.

Over a beer, they asked what there was "to do" in Myrtle Beach. That's when they were told about Georgetown's most famous place, the "Sunset lodge" that, until 1969, operated on Highway 17 just south of Georgetown.

"We were young and foolish, so we decided to take a look," Mr. Sardi said.

It was a brilliant moonlit night, almost as clear as day and, since there didn't seem to be any other vehicular traffic, Mr. Sardi decided to turn his lights off and do some moonlight cruising. Another car, also without lights, rammed them in the rear and they were soon being interviewed by the Georgetown County high sheriff.

The restauranteur reminisced: "He was a true Southern gentleman and his name was…"

He paused, trying to recall it. Knowing something about Georgetown, I volunteered the name of a onetime maintainer of law and order in the Winyah Bay area, a man well-known to everyone in the region at that time.

"That's him," Mr. Sardi exclaimed.

Mr. Sardi continued: "Well, when he found out that both cars were in error and that we, the New York Yankees, had automobile insurance, it put a different light on things and we soon found ourselves at someone's garage where the bent fender and rear bumper could be straightened out."

Then, Mr. Sardi said smilingly, "You'll never believe what happened. When the sheriff found out where we had been heading, he took us out there himself, in his official car and later brought us back to the garage to pick up the convertible. That was a night to remember and he was such a nice gentleman, for a sheriff, that is."

CHRISTMAS EVE

The Georgetown Winyah Gators football team raised money in the mid-1950s to watch the Auburn Tigers play the Vanderbilt Commodores in the Gator Bowl in Jacksonville, Florida. Two players on the team—one a senior and the other the treasurer for the team—went to the Whistling Pig on Christmas Eve to drink a couple of beers. The boy's parents went to church that night followed by a Christmas Eve party. The treasurer had all of the money for the trip in his pocket.

The treasurer leaned over to the senior and quietly suggested it would be a good night to try out the Sunset Lodge. The senior agreed that was an excellent idea.

They never had been to the Sunset Lodge, so they drove south on Highway 17 until the Dutch Colonial house came into view. They drove around the back of the house and knocked on the back door. Hazel opened the door and let them in—on Christmas Eve.

Some people say no one from Georgetown went to the Sunset Lodge, that only men from other cities were customers, but that is not true. The senior barely could think of any friends who did not go there. They paid five dollars each from the Gator Bowl trip money and went upstairs. The senior did not remember much about it; that was a long time ago. He did remember how attractive the girls were. They were dressed in dresses and heels and they wore makeup. Frankly, he considered those women looked better than he and his friend deserved.

They had no business being there.

That was the last time he "went upstairs." He and his friends often went to the Sunset Lodge to play the jukebox and dance with the girls, but he never was a paying customer again. The main concern he and his buddies had hanging around the Sunset Lodge was the possibility of bumping into their dads.

CHARTER BOAT OWNER[72]

A charter boat captain ran a company in the 1950s that had become a booming business. Guys from Columbia and Greenville and Sumter would rent his boat for a few days of fishing, and every night they would go to the Sunset Lodge for the evening. It was the perfect weekend getaway.

Sometimes his customers would go to the Sunset Lodge to drink and dance, and sometimes they would go upstairs with a girl. Most of the men he took fishing considered this trip to Georgetown to be a major expense in their entertainment budget, and they had to spend their money wisely. He worked hard at showing them a good time.

He got to know Hazel pretty well. She noticed when someone brought her repeat business. They flirted a bit. He would tell Hazel his charter business was keeping her brothel in business, and she would say it was more likely her brothel was keeping his charter boat in business. She was correct of course, but they had a lot of fun claiming credit for the success of the other.

He was about Hazel's age; they were in their fifties. Some nights when he did not have a charter, he would show up at the Sunset Lodge later in the evening as men were leaving. He and Hazel would have a couple of drinks and maybe dance a little to the music from the jukebox. Those nights, he stayed with Hazel in her garage apartment. No charge, of course.

STATE SENATOR

I n South Carolina, state senators have a lot of power, particularly in their home districts. The longer a senator has been in office, the more power he or she has, not only near home but statewide. Before 1969, when the Sunset Lodge closed, all state senators were men, as were the news reporters. The men of the press relied on their relationships with the legislators for information to print.

One state senator had been in office for quite some time and had accumulated enough power not to be questioned about what he did with the state plane.

He was a big fan of Hazel Weisse. She made a lot of money in Georgetown with her brothel, and she knew how to take care of men in power. When the state senator called her to meet him in Columbia during the legislative session, she made it her priority to get there. If he told her to bring a couple of girls with her, she did. She was smart. She closed the Sunset Lodge for a week every spring to all customers except legislators and judges. She spent that week meeting the new guys in the legislature and entertaining the guys with seniority.

The men at the statehouse could not wait to head to Georgetown every spring. The legislature did not exactly adjourn that week, but nothing much happened because so many of them were at the Sunset Lodge, and the newspaper reporters did not dare say a word. At the time, there were not many restaurants between Columbia and Georgetown, and they did not want to be seen walking into a restaurant as a group to order lunch, so they took their lunches with them. The good folks at the Palmetto Club would pack twenty-five lunches for those who were heading down to Georgetown, and they would go in cars with two or three in a car.

The truth is, everything at the Sunset Lodge was free that week. Some men would stay down in the living room to listen to the jukebox, dance with the girls and drink liquor, while other men would "go upstairs," as the saying went. Some men stayed at a house on the beach all week, and some men spent one or two nights at a hotel in Georgetown before heading back to Columbia.

One time, the state senator called Hazel to Columbia, and they went to the Palmetto Club to have a few drinks. They started talking about those potato skins with sour cream and cheese and bacon. At that time, the only place you could get such a dish was in New York,[73] and the more they talked about those potato skins, the more they wanted some. The state senator walked into an office at the Palmetto Club and picked up the phone. He called the pilot of the state plane and told him to gas up the plane; he and a guest were flying to New York. He and Hazel drove to the airport and hopped on the plane, and they had a great time. He thought, *What a great girl!*

DEATH[74]

The story is that someone died at the Sunset Lodge one night. It should not be surprising that a man died there; that happens everywhere, even in restaurants. There have been several examples of well-known men in history who have died in awkward circumstances involving women who are not their wives. In this case, the facts have not come out and the story is just rumor.

The rumor is that Hazel called a man to come pick up the deceased, who was stuffed into the kitchen so no one would see him. She and the driver carried the deceased to a car and put him in the trunk, and the man drove away. He drove for hours to put distance between the Sunset Lodge and the place the deceased would be found. He was met by another person who helped move him inside, and then he drove away.

PAWLEYS ISLAND TRIP

There was an in-between age during World War II when some boys were not old enough to join the military but were old enough to enjoy driving cars and having experiences. One group of boys lived in Columbia and loved the Carolina beaches. The challenge was the gas rationing that was started in 1942. Going anywhere took planning and the cooperation of friends.

Gas was rationed by the federal government, not because gas was scarce but because rubber for tires was scarce. Most of the rubber production was in the hands of the bad guys during World War II, and synthetic rubber production was not yet sufficient for the needs of the country. The idea was to reduce rubber tire wear by reducing the availability of gas, and it worked. Most drivers received stamps for three gallons of gas per week unless the owner of the car was a traveling salesman or in another profession that needed to drive for business. Truckers had unlimited access to gas, as did ministers, policemen, firemen and, sadly, two hundred congressmen who took advantage of the system and signed themselves up for unlimited gas.

Three friends wanted to go to Pawleys Island. That is what they told their parents, and that was true. What also was true was their extreme interest in going to the Sunset Lodge, a Georgetown County business about which they had heard much. The challenge they had was getting there. One of the boys had a Model A Ford that could make the trip to Pawleys; his three-gallon stamp would not be enough to get there, but his two buddies and he could arrive in style by combining their stamps. They figured they could get from

SUNSET LODGE IN GEORGETOWN

Columbia to Pawleys on one ten-gallon tank of gas. Then they would need another tank of gas to drive around while there and a third tank for the return trip. By combining three gallons of gas with seven gallons of varsol (a paint thinner that would burn fine in an old Model A as long as it was mixed with enough gas), they could get to Pawleys with one gas stamp.

They left Columbia one morning for Pawleys and were excited. It would be a long day, but that was okay because of the adventures that lay ahead. They had been watching the weather for the last week to make sure the bridge over the Wateree River would be passable. The original road sat on the ground and the bridge was right over the water, so any flooding would have delayed the trip. It was dry as they drove over the wooden plank bridge. There was much that could and did go wrong on a trip that far. The boys knew where the auto repair places were between Columbia and the beach. If they could get to Sumter then they aimed for Manning and then to Cooper's Country Store near Salters on Highway 521 and from there it was not far to Andrews and then to Georgetown. Their big rest stop was in Manning when the engine was hot and tired. They pulled out their sandwiches and ate and rested and waited for the car to cool down enough to unhook the gas line and blow out the carbon build-up. Varsol would run a car, but it was tough on the engine.

They arrived at Pawleys Island in the afternoon. The speed limit was thirty-five miles per hour during the war, so a trip from Columbia to Pawleys Island could be a six- to eight-hour trip if nothing went wrong. Their first order of business was to get a room at the Cassina Inn on the island. The lady who ran the inn rented a half bed for two dollars per night. There were three of them, so she put them in a room with two double beds and charged six dollars per night. The boys were relieved she was not busy; if need be, she would have put another boy in their room in that other half bed. She fed them breakfast and then dinner in the midday, and they were on their own for supper.

The trip to Georgetown County was everything they hoped it would be. They drove to Murrells Inlet and ate at Olivers Lodge one night, and they found the Sunset Lodge the next. The car did great, and they had plenty to talk about on the trip home.

SUNSET LODGE VISIT WORTH IT?

There is a town about an hour from Georgetown, just far enough away to avoid the local awareness of the Sunset Lodge but not too far away to visit from time to time. A group of men had a Saturday routine: cut the grass in the morning and then meet at the barbershop for haircuts and conversation, followed by lunch. There were about a dozen men who would show up on Saturdays, sometimes fewer depending on who had to go out of town or who had a home project to complete; still, it was a good group of guys who knew pretty much everything about one another and everyone else in town. Once they had talked out the issues of the week, they had a variety of options for the rest of the day, including local farm auctions or dinner at the seafood restaurant—or even a visit to the Sunset Lodge.

It was a rainy Saturday and sort of cold. A few men were sitting in the barbershop with not much to do that weekend. Their wives were in Columbia for a Baptist ladies' conference and would be back late. Someone suggested they head down to Georgetown that afternoon for a visit to the Sunset Lodge followed by steaks at the Lafayette Restaurant and back home before their wives returned. Some guys could go and some could not go or did not want to go. Four men were ready to go. They asked one friend if he wanted to go. He asked what time they were heading to Georgetown, and they said about 4:00 p.m. so they would have time to eat dinner in Georgetown before going home. He said no, he did not want to go.

The four of them rode to Georgetown in one car, pulled into the Sunset Lodge driveway at the wagon wheel by the road and parked near the back door. One of the advantages of living an hour away was not having to hide the car in the woods like the locals. They walked up to the back door as their friend who did not want to go to Georgetown walked out.

They stopped to visit a minute and asked him what changed his mind, and he said he did not want to go that late and besides, money was tight and he could not afford to pay for a girl and a steak too. They asked him if the visit to the Sunset Lodge was worth it, and he said it was worth it going in, but he was not so sure coming out.

VISIT TO THE DOCTOR

One of the advantages of living in a small town is easy access to stores and services. Most residents walk everywhere. When one man was very young, living in Georgetown, his doctor's office was just two blocks from his home, and his dentist was nearby as well. His mother often walked her children to the doctor or the dentist or to Front Street to see a movie. This man was the youngest child, and he had siblings much older.

When he was little, he had a check-up scheduled one day with his doctor, so his mom took him by the hand and walked to the doctor's office, signed in and sat in the waiting room. His momma picked up a magazine. The door opened, and the prettiest woman his seven-year-old eyes had ever seen walked in. He could feel his mother tense as she pretended to read her magazine. The lady walked up to the window and was waved through the door and into the back. She came out a bit later, and before leaving, she walked up to the boy's mother and said, "Your son is the best dancer I know."

And she left. The young boy knew she meant his oldest brother, and so did his momma.

His mother was furious. She grabbed his hand, and they walked home as fast as she could; his feet barely touched the ground. She was almost stuttering. He asked her who that lady was, and she said, "She was one of *those* people!"

His mother worked at a nice dress shop in town, and the ladies from the Sunset Lodge knew her, certainly by sight. The young boy did not know at the time that "those people" meant the women from the Sunset Lodge.

He since has learned all about the Sunset Lodge. The madam, Hazel Weisse, worked hard to avoid the situation that happened to his mother. She warned her sporting ladies not to speak to residents. She did not want anyone from town to be embarrassed or to have a reason to want Hazel to shut down. He heard of Hazel getting rid of a girl who got a speeding ticket; he could not imagine how fast she would have fired a girl who spoke to a townswoman that way.

THE WIFE

A woman and her husband lived in Georgetown. As far as she knew, her husband had been faithful to her, but there had been times he had come home late and she knew he had been drinking and she wondered what he had been up to. One night after dinner, he said he was going out to have a drink with friends and would be back in a couple of hours. For some reason, she just did not believe him. There was something in his manner or his clothes or his mood—something that made her think he was going out to the Sunset Lodge. She decided it was time to know.

She waited an hour and then drove down Highway 17 South until she arrived at the Dutch Colonial building on the right of the road, directly across from the airport. She was not sure what to do. There were cars parked in the back, but she did not see his car, so she parked her car so she could see the back of the house. And she waited. After sitting in that car for two hours, she gave up and went home. She must have been wrong, but her instincts were so certain! She looked at every man who walked in the back and every man who walked out, and her guy was not there. Other than looking to see who she knew and making mental notes to pass along some tips to some women she knew, she was excruciatingly bored. The only excitement all night was when some guy died.

About thirty minutes after parking her car, she saw a hearse drive up and park near the back door. That got her attention; at least she had something to watch. Two men hopped out of the car and carried a folded stretcher through the back door. After a few minutes, the door opened, and the two men carried out a body on the stretcher; there was a sheet covering the man. That is too bad, she thought. She had heard exertion could kill a man, but there was little risk of that at her house. When the show was over and the hearse disappeared up Highway 17 North, she really began to get bored. She stuck it out another hour and then decided she was wrong; her husband must have been at a friend's house like he said. She drove home.

The lights were on at the house and his car was not parked at home, but when she walked in, there he was in his bathrobe watching television. She was surprised he was home and she was tired from sitting in the car and she was frustrated that here he was, comfortable. She almost burst into tears when he said in a challenging voice, "Where have you been?"

She barely could process the question and said the only thing that came to mind: "Where have *you* been?"

"My car has been stolen. The sheriff and I have been riding around the last couple of hours looking for it."

That does not make sense, she thought. It just did not ring true.

"Is that so. Let's see what the sheriff says about that."

She called the sheriff's office and asked to speak to the sheriff. She told him who she was and asked him if he had seen her husband that evening.

"Yes, ma'am," he said. "We have been driving around looking for your car, but do not worry, I am sure we will find it in the morning."

She thanked him and hung up. Something was not right, but she could not figure out what it was.

EPILOGUE

S he worked at the Sunset Lodge. She was not proud of what she did, but at that time in her life, she had no marketable skills, she was far from home and she found a job that could make her a lot of money—and she made a lot of money. Hazel was good to her girls. She paid them half of the customer fee and she fed them and kept them at the brothel free of rent, although there came a time when she "charged" them rent; something about IRS rules. One thing they did not have was freedom.

Hazel told them not to go into town in groups of more than two, and they could not speak to any man they saw on the sidewalk. No soliciting! She was serious; she fired one girl who told a lady that her son was a good dancer. The girl was gone that day! Hazel was furious. She got the girls in the dining room and screamed and cussed and wore them out. She said the town tolerated her business because she did not embarrass the residents and because she brought a lot of money to Georgetown. She told them never to speak to a resident of Georgetown again or they would be finding their cute selves driving their fancy new cars on the Coastal Highway out of Georgetown County. She was hot!

The only time the girls went to town was on Monday morning to see the doctor and usually one other day during the week, sometimes with Hazel, sometimes with Hazel's driver or a cab. Monday was doctor day and banking day. They earned a lot of cash on the weekends, and by Monday morning, the risk was too high that another girl would steal some money; it was best to get to the bank.

Most girls put their cash into a savings account; sometimes they bought bonds. The week after arriving in Georgetown, this woman went to town with a couple of girls to see the doctor and then to the bank, where she opened a savings account. Hazel had a PO box that they all used for their official address. She had to use her real name. The doctor visit every Monday did not take long. The nurse made sure they did not have to sit in the waiting room. The doctor did not want them upsetting his patients. The doctor would check over their tests results from the previous week's visit and run new tests, and he would give them certifications of good health that Hazel would put under the glass by their bed at the Sunset Lodge. Hazel told them if they came back from town without that certification of good health then they could just keep going. She required that certification.

There were some nice stores on Front Street. It was fun shopping since she knew she could afford anything she liked. She bought a lot of jewelry, clothes and stuffed animals on Front Street. She bought a car in Georgetown. She bought glasses on Front Street and even books. She loved music, and she bought records and even a guitar. She spent a lot of money. She also mailed money home. Her folks were struggling, and she told them she was a salesperson in a jewelry store and she worked on commission, and when she had a good week, she could send them some money. It would have killed them if they knew what she was doing. She sent her momma some pretty nice jewelry for her birthday and for Christmas, and she sent her daddy a watch and rings. Her sister told her later their parents sold some of the jewelry to make ends meet.

She was grateful the owner of the jewelry store allowed her to pretend she worked there so she could mail packages from the store. Usually the girls who wanted to mail presents home had to send plain boxes in plain wrappers. The owners of stores on Front Street had a supply of plain boxes and plain wrapping paper for the girls of the Sunset Lodge to mail presents home.

She stayed in Georgetown longer than most girls; the normal stay was six months to a year, but she asked Hazel if she could stay. And then Hazel closed the Sunset Lodge; rather, the sheriff closed it down. The girl heard a lot of rumors about how it happened. All she knew was it made her change her life.

She rented a room in Georgetown and tried to figure out what to do next. She could go home, but how awkward would that be to move back with her parents with a savings account with over $10,000 and no discernible skills? She met the owner of a small restaurant in the county, and they started courting. He took her to his church and she worked some at his restaurant, and they fell in love. They got married about a year later. She invested some of the money in her savings account in restaurant equipment, and they improved the quality of the food they served. It was not long before people could not remember when she was not the wife of the restaurant owner.

She worked the front counter most Sundays. They had a big after-church crowd, and it was all hands on deck. Her husband was cooking in the back, and she was taking money in the front. One Sunday, she looked up and saw the sheriff and his wife and another couple walk in and sit down. She sent the waitress over there and told her to take good care of that table. When they finished dinner, she told the waitress not to tell them why but to tell them their ticket had been paid.

It was obvious the sheriff did not like that; she could see him turn on the young fellow who held up his hands and said, "Not me!" The sheriff looked around the room, called the waitress over and demanded his ticket. It was all she could do not to laugh out loud. He was so frustrated! He got up and walked over and told her he wanted his ticket. She said, "Sheriff, you would not recognize me, and I am not willing to discuss it, but thank you. If not for you, I still would be at the Sunset Lodge."

He stood there speechless, processing what she had said. He turned and went to his table.

AFTERWORD

What are we to make of the Sunset Lodge in Georgetown, South Carolina? Clearly, brothels are illegal in most jurisdictions, and the Sunset Lodge was a brothel in conservative and religious Georgetown County in even more conservative and religious South Carolina. How in the world did Hazel Weisse set up a house of prostitution, grow it and maintain it for thirty-three years?

The comment I heard the most from Georgetonians was that Hazel did a good job keeping a low profile. She had excellent business instincts. Her business attracted tourists, she did not embarrass the town, she had a small footprint in the county, she did not use natural resources, she did not ask for tax breaks and her employees spent a lot of money locally. She did not allow her women to solicit business on Front Street, and her brothel was not on anyone's radar screen. And yet, Hazel's name appeared in the *Georgetown Times* as a contributor to local charities. She moved around town freely, everyone knew who she was and the local business community accommodated the needs of her employees. There never was a concerted effort to shut her down.

Did she use her money to buy acceptance? I heard a lot of compliments over my years of research for the role Hazel played as a good corporate citizen. There is no doubt she would have won an award as the Businessperson of the Year had the local chamber of commerce had a category that recognized Best Brothel or even Most Generous Business.

Hazel stayed focused on her primary business purpose and did not get diverted into other products or services; however, I found it interesting that she sold alcohol. Selling liquor and beer was risky, and I wondered if she paid for a liquor license and paid taxes on her sales. Everything I have heard and read about Hazel gives me the impression she did not take chances. The retired IRS agent I interviewed told me Hazel paid every fee and every tax she owed, so I think it likely she reported her alcohol sales.

Writing this book has been about the most fun I have ever had. With an amazing few exceptions, everyone I asked (or Paige Sawyer asked for me) agreed to talk with me about the Sunset Lodge. There is a fascination, and maybe a bit of pride, from the residents of Georgetown County about the Sunset Lodge. It closed fifty years ago, so no one has felt the need to defend what went on there. The storyteller and I would sit down at a restaurant or a home or in a business and visit about Georgetown in the '50s and '60s. It was hard to find anyone who could talk about the '40s, as they were too long ago, but I heard stories about the '40s from the grown children of those who lived it. Sometimes the person had a great story, and sometimes the story was a story I had heard or I realized the story could not have happened, or I knew more about the story than he or she did, but that was okay; hearing stories repeated helped me better understand.

I have spoken to hunting club members, Rotary Clubs, men's societies, book clubs, historical associations, libraries and garden clubs. Each speaking engagement has helped me organize and edit the material for this book. I started the preparation for each speaking invitation with a blank sheet and built the talk from scratch. One recent historical association meeting had an unusually large crowd, and a friend sat in the audience directly in front of two elderly ladies. After I finished my presentation, one turned to the other and said, "I heard him speak at my garden club. It was juicier."

People told me Sunset Lodge stories that I would be embarrassed to repeat, let alone write down. Men have suggested I publish an R-rated and X-rated companion pamphlet to this book and have predicted the pamphlet would outsell the book itself, but I cannot do it. It would be too much.

Brothels exist. One can read about prostitution in the Bible and in today's newspaper. Will there be another Sunset Lodge? Hazel's brothel was remarkable for the length of time it existed in one place and owned by one person, but there was nothing admirable or particularly interesting going on at the Sunset Lodge. She had the perfect business model for that time and place, she developed powerful friends who protected her, she spent money, she gave away money and she managed her employees.

As much fun as I have had interviewing people and researching documents for this book, I have maintained a low-grade uneasiness about the topic of prostitution. I have great admiration for Hazel Weisse's business skill, but I agree with those who are offended by her business. It is not an excuse to do well that which you should not be doing at all. Perhaps other houses of prostitution will find it impossible to stay in business if local laws are vigorously enforced.

NOTES

Author's Narrative

1. Andrew Bernard Harper, Estill, South Carolina (1956–2017).
2. Tom Rubillo, *Georgetown Times*, June 26, 2006.
3. Rebecca T. Godwin, *Keeper of the House* (New York: St. Martin's Press, 1994).
4. There is a persistent rumor that the multicolored light panel over the bar at the private Pine Tree Hunt Club in Columbia, South Carolina, came from the Sunset Lodge. I believe it.
5. *Pretty Woman*, written by J.F. Lawton, produced by Amon Milchan, Steven Reuther and Gary W. Goldstein, directed by Garry Marshall. Touchstone Pictures, 1990.
6. Margaret Mitchell, *Gone with the Wind* (New York: Macmillan, 1936).
7. Eugene N. Zeigler, *Barnwell Blarney or Colonel Frank Remembered* (n.p.: Clio Press Inc., 1999).

Georgetown County, South Carolina

8. Virginia Christian Beach, *Rice and Ducks: The Surprising Convergence that Saved the Carolina Lowcountry* (Charleston, SC: Evening Post Books, 2014), 66. What a magnificent book! This book is a work of art with beautiful photography, stunning artwork and well-researched and interesting writing. Virginia Beach persuasively traced the history of the rise and fall of the rice culture in South Carolina and the process of the transfer of responsibility for the coastal lands to outside influences.
9. Neal Cox, *Neal Cox of Arcadia Plantation: Memoirs of a Renaissance Man* (n.p.: Home House Press, 2003), 27.

10. George C. Rogers Jr., *The History of Georgetown County, South Carolina* (Columbia: University of South Carolina Press, 1970), 324.

11. Arney R. Childs, *Rice Planter & Sportsman: The Recollections of J. Motte Alston, 1821–1909* (Columbia: University of South Carolina Press, 1953), 111.

12. Christian Beach, *Rice and Ducks*, 32.

13. Duncan Clinch Heyward, *Seed from Madagascar* (Chapel Hill: University of North Carolina Press, 1937), 18.

14. Map of Slave Population, compiled from census of 1860, Library of Congress, Call Number G3861.E9 1860.H4.

15. Cornelius O. Cathey, ed., *A Woman Rice Planter: Patience Pennington* (Cambridge, MA: Belknap Press of Harvard University Press, 1961), xxvi.

16. Christian Beach, *Rice and Ducks*, 47.

17. An old story in Georgetown claimed an employee went to his Front Street hardware store owner to confess he could not remember which plantation owner ordered a saddle that had arrived. The owner told him to bill them all and they could determine who ordered the saddle by who paid the bill. They all paid the bill.

18. Christian Beach, *Rice and Ducks*, 23.

19. Bernard M. Baruch, *Baruch: My Own Story* (New York: Henry Holt and Company, 1957), 270–71.

20. Walter Edgar, ed., *South Carolina Encyclopedia* (Columbia: University of South Carolina Press, 2006), 54.

21. *Daily Item*, September 26, 1912. The *Daily Item* was the Georgetown newspaper.

22. Christian Beach, *Rice and Ducks*, 93.

23. *The State*, October 25, 1925.

24. Bill Nowlin, *Tom Yawkey: Patriarch of the Boston Red Sox* (Lincoln: University of Nebraska Press, 2018), 4.

25. Rogers, *History of Georgetown County*, 495. The Carolina Plantation Society still is going strong. I was invited to speak to its society members one spring day a few years ago. The members take turns hosting the society, and the year I spoke, we met under a huge tent in the front yard of a 1930s-era hunting lodge. We enjoyed an hour of refreshments followed by a buffet line of delicious food choices followed by my talk. As is the case in all of my talks to older men and women in South Carolina, there were some there who knew more about the Sunset Lodge than I did.

26. Ibid., 496.

27. *Georgetown Times*, October 16, 1936.

28. Ibid.

29. *Field and Stream*, October 1922, 719. Also involved in advertising in *Field and Stream* from Georgetown were F.E. Johnstone and A. Lambert. Johnstone owned the 5,300-acre Belle Isle Plantation, where he hosted men who stayed for hunting trips. Lambert owned a plantation fourteen miles from Georgetown and advertised, "In the heart of the duck country I furnish comfortable sleeping quarters, best of meals, careful guides, boats and decoys" (*Field and Stream*, November 1922, 814). There was an active effort to pull northern money to Georgetown County.

30. Interview with Lee Gordon Brockington, May 5, 2015.

31. Ronald E. Bridwell, "The Gem of the Atlantic Seaboard," *Georgetown Times*, 1991, 60.

32. Betty Roberson and Betty Williams, "713 Front Street," in *A Walk Down Front Street* (n.p.: Georgetown County Historical Society, 2010).

33. Frances Cheston Train, *A Carolina Plantation Remembered* (Charleston, SC: The History Press, 2008), 66.

Hazel Weisse

34. *Star Press* (Muncie, IN), October 5, 1928.

35. Interview with Bettye Marsh, July 16, 2009.

36. Great American Stations, "Florence, SC (FLO)," www.greatamericanstations.com/stations/FLO/Station_view.

37. Jessie Barnwell was Frank Barnwell's wife. Eugene Zeigler wrote a book about Frank Barnwell in 1999, titled *Barnwell Blarney or Colonel Frank Remembered*, published by Clio Press.

38. *Florence Morning News*, May 15, 1935.

39. *Georgetown Times*, October 16, 1936.

40. Mitchell, *Gone with the Wind*.

41. *Georgetown Times*, 1966.

42. *Georgetown Times*, December 18, 1969.

43. *Charleston News and Courier*, December 14, 1969.

44. *Charleston Evening Post*, December 24, 1969.

45. *The State*, December 17, 1969

46. *The State*, February 29, 1972

Thomas Austin Yawkey

47. Nowlin, *Tom Yawkey*.

48. *New York Times*, March 18, 1919. It has been difficult following the money from William Yawkey to Bill Yawkey and Augusta Austin to Tom Austin

Yawkey and Emma Marie Austin. The inheritances quoted in various sources never add up, so for this purpose, the article in the *New York Times* is a published account. By all accounts, Emma Marie virtually got left out of the inheritance goodies, but at that time, even her pittance made her a wealthy woman.

49. Nowlin, *Tom Yawkey*, 30.

50. Rogers, *History of Georgetown County*, 493.

51. *The State*, October 25, 1925.

52. Nowlin, *Tom Yawkey*, 333.

53. Ibid., 104.

54. Ibid.

55. Interview with Ralph Ford Jr., 2005.

56. Ibid.

57. Steve Williams, *Ebony Effects: 150 Unknown Facts About Blacks in Georgetown, S.C.* (Conway, SC: Waccamaw Press, 2012), 348.

58. Interview with Jeep Ford, 2003.

59. *Georgetown Times*, February 16, 1945.

60. Interview with Phil Wilkinson, 2010.

61. Georgetown Presbyterian Church, *The First Hundred Years, 1897–1997* (Columbia, SC: R.L. Bryan, 1997), 50–51.

62. Letters courtesy of Dewey Ervin of Columbia, South Carolina. Dewey's grandfather was James R. McLeod, the son of the founder of McLeod Hospital and the recipient of the letters from Tom Yawkey.

63. Interview with Phil Wilkinson, 2010.

64. Nowlin, *Tom Yawkey*, 402.

65. Baseball History Blog, "Tom Yawkey's Whorehouse," April 12, 2010.

66. Interview with Phil Wilkinson, 2010.

67. Ibid.

International Paper Employee

68. *Georgetown Times*, July 20, 1987. Interview of Howard Izard by Denise Johnson.

Flower Shop Owners

69. The son of a business owner on Front Street who married in 1970 told almost the identical story. Hazel already had retired. She stopped by the man's store and left $100 for the son as a wedding gift. The son's new mother-in-law saw the gift and asked her daughter who Hazel Weisse was. The son's new wife said, "Um, she is one of Mike's friends."

Bookstore Owner

70. Beth Brown, comp., *All Cats Go to Heaven: An Anthology of Stories About Cats* (New York: Grosset & Dunlap, 1960).

Never Say Sardi

71. Jack Leland with the *Georgetown Times* wrote this article in 1985 about an experience Vincent Sardi claimed to have in Georgetown in the 1930s after graduation from high school.

Charter Boat Owner

72. There is one popular story about a fishing boat owner who traded shad roe for a trip upstairs at the Sunset Lodge. American shad is a bony saltwater fish that spawns in fresh water. With five rivers pouring into the county, the Georgetown area is a perfect breeding ground for shad. The roe is a sack of fish eggs that is removed from the shad and cooked, usually wrapped in bacon, fried and served with grits. The shad roe season is short, about six weeks in the early spring. According to the story, Hazel and several of the sporting ladies ate the shad roe and became violently ill. Hazel told the boat owner he had to pay cash only going forward.

State Senator

73. The part about flying to New York to eat potato skins was not true. They may have taken the state plane to see a Red Sox game or eat at Sardi's or tour the Statue of Liberty but not eat potato skins. Richard Melman opened R.J. Grunts in 1971 in Chicago, and he is credited with developing potato skins for the menu. The Sunset Lodge closed in 1969, two years earlier.

Death

74. There is a persistent rumor of a death at the Sunset Lodge—not just anyone, but someone important. There is nothing published, just rumor.

ABOUT THE AUTHOR

D avid Gregg Hodges lives in Columbia, South Carolina. He has been married to Susan Graybill Hodges since 1975 and has four children and nine grandchildren, all of whom live in Columbia. He has been an insurance agent since 1977 and continues to work full time in the life insurance industry. He is a collector of South Carolina books and used to own a used and rare bookstore, the Book Place, in Columbia. He is active in community affairs by serving on local and state charitable boards. His e-mail address is dghodges@aol.com.